COUNTRIES OF THE WORLD

Saudi Arabia

Gareth Stevens Publishing
A WORLD ALMANAC EDUCATION GROUP COMPANY

About the Author: Dynise Balcavage is a freelance writer and the author of six other books. She has visited many foreign lands, including Syria, Jordan, Israel, Morocco, and Turkey, and has spent a great deal of time in France. Balcavage lives in Philadelphia with her husband, cat, and two birds.

Written by
DYNISE BALCAVAGE

Edited by
YUMI NG

Edited in the U.S. by
PATRICIA LANTIER
MONICA RAUSCH

Designed by
JAILANI BASARI

Picture research by
SUSAN JANE MANUEL

Updated and Reprinted in 2002
First published in North America in 2001 by
Gareth Stevens Publishing
A World Almanac Education Group Company
330 West Olive Street, Suite 100
Milwaukee, Wisconsin 53212 USA

Please visit our web site at:
www.garethstevens.com
For a free color catalog describing
Gareth Stevens' list of high-quality books
and multimedia programs, call
1-800-542-2595 (USA) or
1-800-461-9120 (CANADA).
Gareth Stevens Publishing's
Fax: (414) 332-3567.

© **TIMES MEDIA PRIVATE LIMITED 2001**
Originated and designed by
Times Editions
An imprint of Times Media Private Limited
A member of the Times Publishing Group
Times Centre, 1 New Industrial Road
Singapore 536196
http://www.timesone.com.sg/te

Library of Congress Cataloging-in-Publication Data
Balcavage, Dynise.
Saudi Arabia / by Dynise Balcavage.
p. cm. — (Countries of the world)
Includes bibliographical references and index.
ISBN 0-8368-2338-9 (lib. bdg.)
1. Saudi Arabia—Juvenile literature. [1. Saudi Arabia.] I. Title.
II. Countries of the world (Milwaukee, Wis.)
DS204.25.B35   2001
953.8—dc21   2001020233

Printed in Malaysia

2 3 4 5 6 7 8 9 05 04 03 02

Contents

AN OVERVIEW OF SAUDI ARABIA

A land of kings and camels, desert nomads and oil wells, the Kingdom of Saudi Arabia boasts a rich and intriguing history and landscape. Since the country is still fairly difficult to visit — only Muslims making the *hajj* (HYE-ch), a religious pilgrimage, or travelers with Saudi sponsors are easily granted entry into the country — the kingdom continues to mystify travelers and scholars.

Saudi Arabia is the birthplace of Islam. The kingdom houses two of Islam's holiest cities, Mecca and Medina. Each year, Muslims from all over the world flock to these holy sites.

Saudi Arabia has changed quite a bit over the past decades. Still, despite its modern conveniences, the Kingdom of Saudi Arabia remains deeply rooted in its tradition and history.

Opposite: **The Clock Tower in Riyadh displays the emblem of Saudi Arabia: a date palm, which stands for vitality and growth, at the center and two crossed daggers, which represent justice and strength rooted in faith, below.**

Below: **All devout Muslims, including young Saudis like these boys, try to make the hajj pilgrimage at least once in their lives.**

THE FLAG OF SAUDI ARABIA

Saudi Arabia's flag was adopted in 1973. The flag was originally a *Wahhabi* (wah-HAH-bee) banner. The Wahhabis are an Islamic sect that believes in a literal interpretation of the *Qur'an* (kor-AHN). The banner consists of two white images on an emerald green background. The white Arabic script on the flag translates as: "There is no God but Allah and Muhammad is His Prophet." Saudi flags are sewn so viewers can read the message correctly from both sides. An unsheathed sword sits below the words. Out of respect for the script, Saudis never fly their flag at half-mast.

Geography

The largest country in the Middle East, Saudi Arabia covers about four-fifths of the Arabian peninsula and is about one-fourth the size of the United States. The kingdom's location at the junction of three continents — Europe (by way of the Suez Canal), Asia, and Africa — makes Saudi Arabia an important crossroad.

The Red Sea forms Saudi Arabia's western border, and the Persian Gulf borders the country to the east. Neighboring countries to the south include Yemen and the Sultanate of Oman. To the east are the United Arab Emirates, Qatar, and the island state of Bahrain. Kuwait, Iraq, and Jordan border the country in the north.

The kingdom's area is about 865,000 square miles (2,240,350 square kilometers). Only the northern borders, the Qatar border, the Oman border, and a section of the Yemen border are clearly marked and measured.

A Country of Deserts

From deserts to green mountains, from steep cliffs to sparkling coastlines, Saudi Arabia boasts a variety of land features.

THE BEDOUIN

The Bedouin are desert nomads — people who move from place to place, taking their herds in search of pastures. The Bedouin have roamed the deserts of Saudi Arabia and the Middle East since ancient times.
(A Closer Look, page 44)

Below: **A gravel desert meets sandy dunes in the western part of Saudi Arabia.**

Left: **The Asir region, nicknamed the "garden of Saudi Arabia" because it receives the most rain, boasts spectacular mountain scenery.**

Most of the country, however, is blanketed with deserts. The world's largest sand desert, the *Rub Al-Khali* (roob ahl-HAH-lee), or Empty Quarter, covers about half of Saudi Arabia. The northwest area of Saudi Arabia contains another large sand desert, the An-Nafud, which stretches into Iraq. Here, hardy shrubs form a patchy cover over the barren soil. The Eastern Province is covered with salt flats, or *sabkha* (SOB-hah). In the center of this province, the Al-Hasa Oasis gleams like a jewel.

Mountains and Canyons

A mountain chain runs across the western end of Saudi Arabia, and, as the mountains approach Yemen to the south, they rise in elevation and become larger. Many of Saudi Arabia's tourist areas are located in this region, which is called Asir.

Climate

With less than 5 inches (13 centimeters) of rain each year, Saudi Arabia is one of the world's most arid countries. The four seasons are not clearly defined in Saudi Arabia, but the winter months (from October to May) are marked by cool, rainy weather.

Summers are usually hot, with temperatures rising to 120° Fahrenheit (49° Celsius) in some areas. During winter, temperatures can dip down to 74° F (23° C) in Jiddah, 58° F (14° C) in Riyadh, and below freezing in the central and northern parts of the country.

Although the Empty Quarter might not have rain for a decade, the southern Asir mountains might receive up to 10 inches (25 cm) of rain each year due to summer monsoons. Winds blowing from the northwest can also generate sandstorms in the desert, which can drastically reduce visibility.

Water

In a country as dry as Saudi Arabia, finding enough water for the population was a real challenge until the government built desalination facilities. These facilities remove the salt from sea water and make it suitable for drinking and bathing.

Below: Sabkha, or salt flats, were formed when the water from lakes evaporated. Sabkha are most common in the Eastern Province.

Most of Saudi Arabia's fresh water remains hidden beneath the ground. In the eastern part of the country and in the Jabal Tuwayq Mountains, many underground artesian wells exist.

A Wealth of Natural Resources

Mineral resources are abundant in Saudi Arabia. The kingdom is the Middle East's largest oil producer. Numerous other minerals exist, including gold, silver, iron, copper, zinc, manganese, tungsten, lead, sulfur, phosphate, soapstone, asbestos, and feldspar. Since oil is much more profitable, however, these minerals have not been harvested extensively.

Wildlife

Despite their arid climate, the Saudi deserts abound with colorful plant and animal life, particularly after a rainstorm. Desert chamomile, scarlet pimpernel, heliotrope, and wild iris dot the terrain. Still, owing to the dry conditions, only about one percent of Saudi Arabian land is used for farming. Saudi farmers grow date palms, figs, and carob, among other fruits and vegetables.

Lizards, porcupines, hedgehogs, and rabbits are among the animals that scurry across the dunes. Camels, ibex, oryx, sand cats, hyenas, and even baboons also make their homes in Saudi Arabia. Scorpions and cobras also live in the kingdom. Their stings and bites are poisonous and can kill humans and other animals.

THE CAMEL

Camels are useful to desert dwellers in a variety of ways. Their strong and sturdy bodies make them suitable for transporting people and heavy baggage in harsh desert conditions. Their milk is highly nutritious and even contains vitamin C.

(A Closer Look, page 46)

9

History

Ancient Times

Ancient Saudi history is somewhat difficult to uncover, partly because the desert's sands have probably buried much of the country's archaeological treasures. Historians do know, however, that the first Saudis were probably members of the Minaean kingdom. These wandering nomads lived in southwestern Arabia during the twelfth century B.C.

The first settlements appeared in the fertile southwestern part of the Arabian peninsula. The people of the Sabaean or Saba' kingdom cultivated the land and built dams to irrigate their crops. The Sabaean kingdom, which lasted from about 800 B.C. to A.D. 200, was eventually conquered by the Himyarite kingdom, a group of people who lived at the southwestern tip of the Arabian peninsula. By the third century, the southern kingdoms, for the most part located in present-day Yemen, were somewhat unified.

Below: **The cave tombs at Madain Saleh, built almost two thousand years ago, have stood the test of time.**

From about 300 B.C. to A.D. 100, the Nabataeans settled in northwestern Saudi Arabia. They are best known for the many magnificent cities that they carved out of sandy rocks and cliffs. Visitors can still see their handiwork in Madain Saleh.

Because of their location near the trade routes, these small kingdoms earned their living by collecting tolls and offering protection to traders who passed through their land. Cities such as Mecca and Medina developed along these trade routes.

In the northwest, by the end of the sixth century, the Hijaz region had become an important stop along a major trade route from Egypt and the Byzantine Empire to India. Merchants bought and sold silk, spices, and sweet-smelling frankincense and myrrh, which the Egyptians used to embalm their dead. They also traded animal skins, ivory, and Arabian gold and gemstones.

The harsh desert landscape largely molded the lifestyle of the early Arabs. Some settled near oases and became farmers. Others, the ancestors of the Bedouin, became nomads and led their herds of sheep and goats across the desert.

Above: **The palace of Ibn Madi in Najran, built in the seventeenth century, has been restored to its original grandeur.**

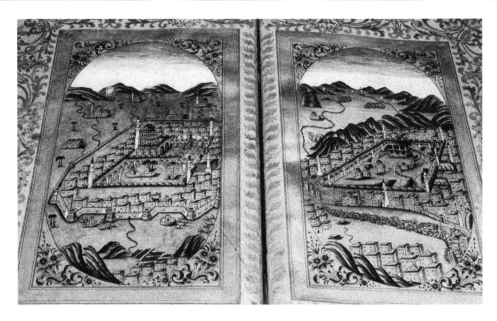

Islam Shapes the Arabian Peninsula

When the prophet Muhammad was born in Mecca in the sixth century A.D., his hometown was already a sacred place where people worshiped pagan gods. Muhammad founded Islam in 622 in Medina, and converted the people of Mecca soon after. From these two cities, the Islamic religion spread to Spain and India and on to central Asia. Muhammad founded a Muslim empire in Mecca that continued to grow until about 750, although the religious center moved from Medina to Damascus, Syria, in 661.

By the eighth century, Arabia was no longer an important political force. Arabian tribes were split into warring factions, and Arabia was controlled by numerous groups. In the early 1500s, the Ottoman Turks conquered parts of western Arabia, but local leaders still ruled most of the inland region.

In the eighteenth century, a religious leader named Abd Al-Wahhab revolutionized Islam by preaching a return to the original teachings of the prophet Muhammad. Although the religion he taught was very strict, Al-Wahhab had the support of the powerful Al-Saud clan that led Arabia at that time, and many more people joined Islam. As the movement spread, tribes began to unite and occupy parts of Arabia under the leadership of the Al-Saud family. The Ottomans fought against this expansion, however, and civil war among the tribes also weakened local power. By 1891, control over most of Arabia was once again divided among various tribal chiefs and the Ottomans.

ISLAM IN SAUDI ARABIA

As the birthplace of Islam, Saudi Arabia houses Islam's holiest city, Mecca. Islam is the kingdom's official religion, and it is against the law to practice any other religion within Saudi Arabia's borders.

(A Closer Look, page 56)

At the beginning of World War I (1914–1918), the Ottoman Turks controlled western Arabia and had the support of the Al-Rashid tribe in central and northern Arabia. Abdul Aziz Ibn Saud, a member of the Al-Saud clan who had been in exile in Kuwait, and his Wahhabi followers occupied Riyadh and eastern Arabia. With the help of the British, Ibn Saud then drove the Turks from all of Arabia and united the country. In 1932, Ibn Saud became the father of the Kingdom of Saudi Arabia.

Left: **Abdallah Ibn Saud, a member of the powerful Al-Saud clan, was the leader of the Wahhabis during the 1750s.**

LAWRENCE OF ARABIA

Thomas E. Lawrence was born in Wales but is known to the world as "Lawrence of Arabia." He helped the Arabs win back their land from the Ottoman Turks during World War I.
(A Closer Look, page 60)

A Time of Change

Since the kingdom was officially founded in 1932, various members of Ibn Saud's family have ruled Saudi Arabia and have worked to make it one of the world's wealthiest nations.

Oil was discovered in the 1930s during Ibn Saud's reign. Under his leadership, by the 1950s, the kingdom was earning about $1 million a week from its oil production. Today, the country's oil industry brings in about $315 million a day!

When Ibn Saud died, his son, Saud, became the country's new leader in 1953. While Saud was leader, Saudi Arabia helped its neighbor, Yemen, fight a civil war against Egyptian-backed forces from 1962 to 1967. In 1964, however, the Al-Saud family council met and decided to replace Saud with his brother Faisal.

Over the next few decades, Saudi Arabia had several kings. After Faisal became king in 1964, he worked hard to modernize Saudi Arabia by implementing the first in a series of five-year development plans. His reign, however, was cut short when a deranged nephew assassinated him in 1975. Khalid, Faisal's half-brother, then became the new ruler.

Khalid's reign brought great challenges. In 1979, a group of three hundred radicals took over Mecca's Grand Mosque. Government troops finally regained control of the mosque after ten days, but, in the process, more than 250 people lost their lives. In 1982, after King Khalid's death, Crown Prince Fahd became the country's new leader, and he still rules today.

King Fahd is known for his wise business decisions and his friendships with the West. The alliances he developed with Western countries such as the United States, Britain, and France have proven to be valuable. In 1990, Iraq invaded Saudi Arabia's tiny neighbor, Kuwait. A few days later, King Fahd allowed U.S. troops into the kingdom to help defend the country.

King Fahd also helped form a Consultative Council, *Majlis Al-Shura* (MITE-jlees ahl-SHOE-rah), with members appointed by the king. Although this council has no lawmaking powers, it continues to serve as a forum to discuss important issues.

King Fahd helped expand access to the kingdom's holy sites at Mecca and Medina to more Muslims from around the world. The Grand Mosque in Mecca can now hold more than one million worshipers, and the Prophet's Mosque can now accommodate more than half a million Muslims.

Above: **Crown Prince Abdullah is next in line to the Saudi throne.**

SAUDI COURTS

The Council of Ministers and the king are responsible for making the laws and enforcing them in the kingdom. The Saudi court system has four branches. The General Court handles personal, civil, family, or criminal cases; the Limited Court deals with smaller cases involving civil or criminal matters; the Court of Appeals handles appeals, or cases that must be tried in court one more time; and the Supreme Judicial Council handles only matters referred by the king. It also rules on appeals from other courts. Saudi courts have no juries.

King Abdul Aziz Ibn Saud (c. 1880–1953)

On January 15, 1902, the young prince Abdul Aziz Ibn Saud attacked the walled city of Riyadh with the help of about forty soldiers. After conquering the town's forces, he announced that his people, the Al-Saud, were the leaders of Riyadh and central Arabia. Within just three decades, Ibn Saud's reign extended from the Persian Gulf to the Red Sea, and he transformed his kingdom into a modern nation. In 1932, the Kingdom of Saudi Arabia was established.

King Abdul Aziz Ibn Saud

King Faisal (c. 1906–1975)

Faisal Bin Abdul Aziz was crowned king of Saudi Arabia in 1964. Largely responsible for modernizing the kingdom, he spent a great deal of time nurturing relationships with foreign countries, especially with other Islamic nations.

In 1970, King Faisal started the first five-year development plan that spearheaded Saudi Arabia's rapid growth. He also helped foster unity between Islamic countries by helping to create the Organization of the Islamic Conference in Jiddah in 1970. In 1975, *Time* magazine named him the "Man of the Year."

King Faisal

King Fahd (1923–)

The current leader of Saudi Arabia, King Fahd, became ruler when King Khalid died in 1982. King Fahd had a great deal of practice running the country before he was crowned. He had served as the country's first Minister of Education, and, since King Khalid was ill during much of his reign, Fahd had essentially run the country during Khalid's sickness.

King Fahd has also concentrated on developing the economy and alliances with Western countries. In 1993, shortly after the Persian Gulf War, King Fahd formed a Consultative Council, probably in response to criticism that he did not consult with his government advisors before allowing U.S. troops to enter the kingdom.

Over the past few years, however, King Fahd has been ill, and Crown Prince Abdullah has been responsible for many of King Fahd's duties.

King Fahd

Government and the Economy

Government

Saudi Arabia is a hereditary monarchy. The king is the undisputed chief of state and head of government. The Saudi royal family is the most important political group in the kingdom, and leading Saudi princes select the king from the royal family. Their choice, however, must be approved by the *ulema* (oo-leh-MAH), a group of Muslim religious leaders. The king runs the country according to Islamic law, or *shari'a* (shah-REE-ah), which is based on the Qur'an. A Council of Ministers appointed by the king helps the monarch run the government. Governors, also appointed by the king, oversee each of the thirteen provinces. Local tribal leaders also play an important role in government, since many Saudis still display a strong allegiance to their tribes.

RIYADH

Riyadh is the capital city of Saudi Arabia. Despite its humble beginnings, it has grown to become one of the Middle East's most important cities.
(A Closer Look, page 66)

Left: The exterior design of King Fahd's Palace in Riyadh displays traditional Arab architecture, with its windows shaped like keyholes, pointed arches, and domed roofs.

Law

Unlike the Western legal systems, Saudi law does not base punishments on past judgments. Each case is decided in and of itself and has no effect on future cases. Religious courts base all decisions on Islamic law. A judge presides over each court, but there are no juries. The king is the highest court of appeal. Since Saudis believe that only Allah is great, the people consider themselves their king's equals.

The Saudi justice system has been harshly criticized by many human rights groups, including Amnesty International. They have alleged that Saudi Arabia practices torture and arbitrary arrests. Every Friday, the Muslim holy day, criminals and murderers are publicly executed in Riyadh's main square. The punishment for stealing sometimes is the amputation of a hand, but usually only after a thief commits the crime several times.

In spite of the harsh justice system, Saudis have real access to their leaders. During *majlis* (MITE-jlees), which are audiences with local leaders, governors, or even the king, individuals can meet with their leaders to discuss issues or to petition them. The kingdom also uses a grievance board made up of both secular and shari'a-trained lawyers to deal with complaints made against government agencies and their regulations.

Above: **Public corporal punishment in Saudi Arabia serves two purposes: to punish the criminal and to discourage citizens from breaking the law.**

JIDDAH

The second largest city in Saudi Arabia, Jiddah is located on the western coast of the country, facing the Red Sea. The city has been called the "Bride of the Sea" because of its role as the kingdom's main seaport and also because of its great natural beauty.
(A Closer Look, page 58)

Oil

Saudi Arabia is the largest oil producer in the Middle East. In fact, the kingdom contains more than 25 percent of the world's known reserves — about 261 billion barrels! Crude oil and petroleum products make up about 90 percent of the government's export income, and the government has poured most of its profits right back into the oil industry. Over the past few decades, the government has developed several cities, such as Yanbu Al-Bahr on the Red Sea and Al-Jubayl on the Persian Gulf, into important industrial centers where many Saudis have moved to find work.

Though oil is Saudi Arabia's most important and plentiful natural resource, it is not the only resource that contributes to the kingdom's economy. Deposits of other minerals, such as gold, silver, iron, copper, zinc, manganese, tungsten, lead, sulfur, phosphate, soapstone, asbestos, and feldspar, are scattered throughout the country. Compared to the oil industry, however, the profits made from the extraction of these minerals are small.

Above: **The oil refinery at Ras Tanura, near the Persian Gulf, is the largest oil refinery in the world.**

OIL

Geologists found huge underground pools of crude oil in Saudi Arabia in the 1930s. Since then, its systematic exploitation has made Saudi Arabia the largest exporter of oil in the world, as well as a very wealthy nation.
(A Closer Look, page 62)

Other Industries

Saudi Arabia is among the world's largest producers of dates. Saudi farmers also grow wheat, rice, alfalfa, barley, and grapes. Some farmers raise cotton and melons. Saudi-made products include iron and steel, cement, electrical equipment, and processed foods.

The cities of Mecca, Medina, and Jiddah earn much of their income from tourists, since about two million religious pilgrims make the hajj each year.

Saudi Workforce

The Saudi economy relies heavily on foreign labor. Men and women from all over the world come to work temporarily in Saudi Arabia, since the wages are usually very good. They work in many fields, such as medicine, engineering, and teaching. Saudi women are also joining the workforce, and their contributions are essential to the kingdom's development. Many women run their own businesses, including private schools, shops, and sports clubs. Recently, many branches of government, including the Bureau of Civil Services and the Ministry of Foreign Affairs, have opened separate branches that employ women.

THE DATE PALM

Saudi Arabia is one of the world's leading exporters of dates. The date palm is a Saudi symbol and part of the country's national emblem. Saudis enjoy dates in many ways — in desserts, with rice, and as a substitute for sugar in drinks.
(A Closer Look, page 48)

Below: **In many areas of the country, skilled and daring Saudi farmers still harvest dates by hand.**

People and Lifestyle

A Patchwork of Peoples

Saudi Arabia has a diverse population. Of the country's 22 million people, about 16.5 million are citizens of the kingdom. About 82 percent of the kingdom's people have a Saudi Arab background; about 10 percent are Yemeni Arabs; while about 3 percent come from other Arab countries in Africa and Asia. The rest are mainly workers and their families from many different countries — including the United States, Egypt, Korea, Pakistan, and the Philippines — who are temporarily in the kingdom.

Because a diverse group of pilgrims has visited Mecca over the past 1,400 years, the people who live in the Hijaz area, along the western coast, come from many different backgrounds, including Turkish, Iranian, Indonesian, Indian, and African. This region is close to Africa, and the area's architecture reflects African influence. The houses along the Tihamah coast are cone-shaped and are surrounded by fences made from tall grasses, just as houses are in nearby Africa. All Saudis, nevertheless, share the Arabic language and Islamic religion.

Left: Houses along the Tihamah coast reflect African influence. Women decorate the interior walls with colorful designs.

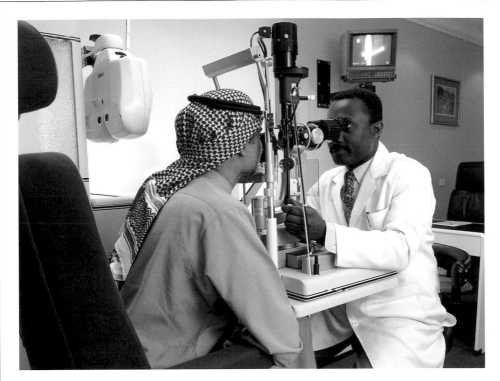

Left: Saudi medical facilities are among the most advanced in the world, and medical care is given free of charge to all Saudi citizens.

A Typical Work Week

Although some women in Saudi Arabia work, most women stay at home to take care of their families and do household chores. Most men work from about 7 a.m. until about 1 p.m. A few more hours of work follow a long break in the afternoon. The work week lasts from Saturday until Wednesday, and the Saudi "weekend" falls on Thursday and Friday. Since Friday is the Muslim holy day, virtually all businesses stay closed on this day. During daily prayer times, all businesses in the kingdom close for anywhere from twenty minutes to one hour.

Staying Healthy

The quality of life for most Saudis remains relatively good. They enjoy a high standard of health care, which is provided to citizens and to religious pilgrims free of charge. The kingdom houses modern hospitals, although the rural areas have fewer medical facilities than the cities. The King Faisal Specialist Hospital and Research Centre is one of the world's most advanced hospitals.

Even with all of the advances in medical technology, however, the average life span in Saudi Arabia is shorter than in many other countries. Men in the kingdom live to be about sixty-six years old, while women live to be about sixty-nine.

GAHWA

Making, pouring, and drinking *gahwa* (GAH-hwah), or Saudi Arabian coffee, is an ancient tradition. A Saudi host usually welcomes guests to his home by pouring a cup of gahwa for each guest with elaborate ceremony.
(*A Closer Look,* page 52)

Left: **Saudi men like to relax by chatting over a cup of coffee or tea.**

WOMEN IN SAUDI ARABIA

The life of a Saudi Arabian woman is largely shaped by the laws of Islam. Her primary role in life is to serve as a good wife and mother, although this role is slowly changing.
(A Closer Look, page 72)

Family Life

Saudi Arabian families are very close and are usually large. The average family has 6.38 children. The oldest male is considered the head of the family, and other members stand by all his decisions. Most social activities occur within the family.

Most Saudis do not choose their spouses. Parents still arrange most marriages. A Saudi man is allowed to have as many as four wives, but most Saudi men have only one. Since the family is the backbone of Saudi Arabian society, divorces are not common, although both men and women can initiate divorces.

It is not uncommon for several generations of a family to live in the same house, and extended families sometimes connect their homes, forming a family compound. The walls of these large family compounds keep out the harsh desert winds. As is the case with most Muslims, Saudis show great respect for the elderly. In fact, caring for elderly parents is considered an honor.

Homes are typically decorated with carpets, etched bronze coffee pots, and small ornaments. Family members usually sit on the floor on carpets to eat. The Saudi version of a sofa is a set of soft pillows that rests on the floor.

Following Islamic tradition, women and girls live in separate rooms from the men and eat in a separate area. This custom, however, is in the process of changing, especially in the cities.

Below: **Saudi women usually marry at a young age, and most stay at home to look after their children.**

Dress

By Western standards, Saudi Arabian clothes might seem conservative. These clothes, however, not only follow Islam's rules of modesty, they also keep Saudis comfortable in every kind of weather, from hot days and cool nights to stinging sandstorms.

Saudi men wear a long, white robe called a *thobe* (THOE-b), regardless of their social status or wealth. Sometimes when the weather is cool, men put a *mishlah* (meesh-LAH-hah), a long, white, brown, or black, gold-trimmed cloak, over their thobes. Men also wear a small skullcap on their heads, called the *tagia* (tahg-EE-ah), over which they drape the *gutra* (GOH-trah), a veil-like head cloth. During the summer, men wear a white gutra. During winter, they change to a warmer, red-and-white checked version. A double cord called an *agal* (oh-GAHL) holds the gutra in place. This cord traditionally was used to lead camels.

Women wear a long, black gown and veil called an *abayah* (ah-BYE-ah) when they go out in public or are near men who are not their close relatives. This garment completely covers their hair and bodies. At home, however, many Saudi women wear stylish Western clothing. Although non-Muslim women who live in the kingdom are not required to don the abayah, they must also wear veils and modest clothes when they go out in public.

Above: **Islamic law forbids Saudi women to uncover their heads and bodies in public places. In some more conservative cities, such as Mecca, women must also cover their faces, leaving only the eyes exposed.**

Left: **A Saudi man sews a mishlah — an Arab-style "overcoat" worn by men in the kingdom.**

Education

While education is not required in Saudi Arabia, it is free to all citizens. Most Saudis attend kindergarten at age six, followed by six years of elementary school, three years of middle school, and three years of high school. Students can choose to attend either vocational or liberal arts and science high schools. All children wear uniforms to school, and boys and girls attend separate schools. The first girls' school in the kingdom was built in 1964.

More boys than girls attend school, since many Saudi families still believe girls do not need an advanced education to perform their traditional roles as future wives and mothers. Today, however, more families are allowing their daughters to pursue a higher education.

Sultana Ali Riza is the founder of the Jiddah Institute for Speech and Hearing (JISH). Three of her four children were born hearing impaired, and she founded JISH so that other hearing-impaired Saudis would not have to face the same problems her children faced. Through the organization, she has created scholarships with San Jose University in the United States, through which Saudi and Arab medical professionals can receive needed training.

Below: **The traditional role of women as housewives and mothers is changing in Saudi Arabia as more opportunities are becoming available for women in education and the workplace.**

Above: **Education is free in Saudi Arabia, and students have access to the latest learning equipment.**

Saudi students must take exams twice a year to test their knowledge. Students receive personalized attention, since there is one teacher for every fifteen or so students — one of the best teacher-to-student ratios in the world.

The kingdom has eight universities, where men and women attend separate classes. About five thousand Saudi Arabians, particularly boys, choose to study in the United States each year. Additionally, the kingdom has developed educational institutions throughout the world for Saudi schoolchildren whose parents work abroad.

The Special Education Department of the Ministry of Education also runs schools for blind, deaf, and physically and mentally disabled people.

Children and young people are not the only ones who can pursue an education in the kingdom. In an effort to wipe out illiteracy, Saudi Arabia has created almost 2,500 adult education centers, where adults can learn to read, write, or improve their skills. These schools have been extremely successful. A few generations ago, only 20 percent of the people in the kingdom could read. Today, about 63 percent of Saudi Arabians are literate.

Left: **The practice of Islam is a part of every Saudi's daily life, along with working, studying, and resting.**

Religion

The world has three major monotheistic religions, or religions that worship one god: Islam, Christianity, and Judaism. Islam is the official religion of the Kingdom of Saudi Arabia, and its beliefs direct every aspect of Saudi law, government, and culture. In fact, people are not allowed to practice any religion other than Islam in the kingdom. This rule does not pose much of a problem, since less than 2 percent of those who live in the kingdom — mostly foreign workers — are not Muslims.

Muslims believe in one God, Allah, and in his prophet, Muhammad. Muslims also believe in other prophets, including Adam, Noah, Isaac, Joseph, Job, Aaron, Solomon, Elias, Jonah, and Jesus, although only Shiite Muslims worship these prophets. Many of these prophets also figure prominently in Christianity and Judaism. In fact, all three monotheistic religions share the same beginnings: they all stem from the prophet Abraham.

Just like Jews and Christians, Muslims believe that life on Earth prepares them for the afterlife. Muslims feel there will be a Day of Judgment when the good and evil people will be separated by God. They also believe in heaven and hell.

When a Muslim dies, a family member usually washes the body and wraps it in a clean, white cloth. The dead are usually buried on the same day that they die, after a prayer service.

About 90 percent of Saudis are Sunni Muslims, while the remaining 10 percent are Shiite Muslims. Most Shiite Muslims live in the Eastern Province.

Qur'an

The Qur'an is the holy book of Islam. Muslims believe it records the exact words revealed by God (Allah) through the angel Gabriel to the prophet Muhammad. Muhammad memorized the message and recited it to his companions. Scribes then wrote down his words.

Perhaps the most amazing fact about the Qur'an is that not a single word in its 114 chapters, or *sura* (SOO-rah), has ever been changed since it was first written. Still, changes in language and beliefs that have occurred over the centuries have led to debate over how the Qur'an should be interpreted.

Matawwa: The Religious Police

The *matawwa* (moo-TAH-wear) are religious police who patrol the streets of Saudi Arabia to make sure people are obeying the laws of Islam. They make sure people dress modestly and shops close for prayer times. Sometimes, members of the Committee for the Preservation of Virtue and the Prevention of Vice enter people's homes.

THE HAJJ PILGRIMAGE

All Muslims are bound by the laws described in the Five Pillars of Islam. The Fifth Pillar is the hajj, or pilgrimage to the holy sites of Mecca and Medina. Recent improvements in the organization of the pilgrimage have made this once-perilous journey safe and possible for Muslims of all ages and walks of life.

(A Closer Look, page 54)

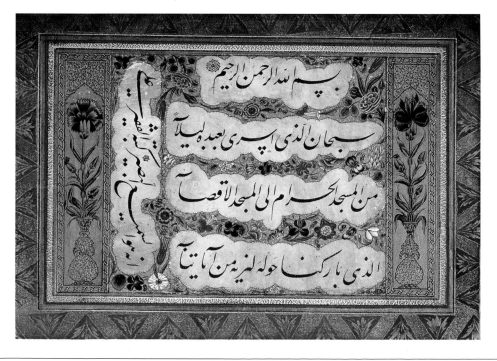

Left: The teachings of the Qur'an form the foundation of the Muslim faith. Gorgeously handwritten manuscripts of the book are precious and are handed down from one generation to the next.

Language and Literature

With its long, curling letters and graceful series of dots and accents, Arabic script is beautiful to look at. People in Saudi Arabia speak Arabic, one of the United Nations' official languages and the official language of the kingdom. Many Saudis, however, conduct business in English.

Arabic has strongly influenced other languages, including Spanish and English. The English language has about six hundred words with Arabic roots, including *sofa*, *average*, *algebra*, *alcove*, *admiral*, *caravan*, *cotton*, *tariff*, *sugar*, *giraffe*, and *arsenal*.

Arabic is read from right to left. Its alphabet has twenty-eight consonants and three vowels. Arabic letters are written differently depending on where they are located — at the beginning, middle, or end of a word. Only long vowels are written out; short vowels are indicated by accent marks placed above or below the consonants. Numbers are also written using this script.

Below: Saudi boys and girls are taught in separate classrooms. Here, schoolboys share a laugh while looking at a picture book.

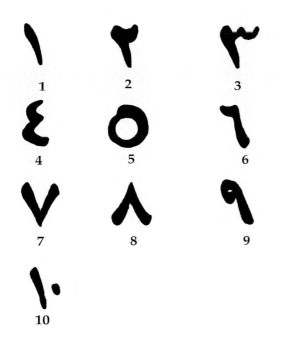

Skilled Poets

Being able to speak well is a respected talent in Saudi Arabia. Perhaps this tradition of public speaking began with the kingdom's poets. Some early Saudi tribesmen believed only three situations in life deserved congratulations: the birth of a son; the birth of a foal, or young horse; and the emergence of a new poet.

Today, the tradition of passing on poems still exists, especially within the Bedouin tribes. The main work of Arabic literature is, of course, the Qur'an, which continues to inspire many writers and poets and is used as the model for all art forms in Saudi Arabia.

Keeping Informed in the Kingdom

The Saudi Arabian Ministry of Information oversees all radio and television services and broadcasts. Saudi Arabian television consists of two channels. One broadcasts in Arabic, while the other offers programs in English and a news bulletin in French. People from nearby countries also have access to these programs. Saudis can hear radio broadcasts in several other languages.

Ten daily newspapers, three English-language papers, and numerous magazines are published in the country. All these publications are censored by the government, however, to ensure that they conform to Islamic teaching.

THE ORYX

The oryx is an antelopelike creature native to the Arabian peninsula and other parts of the Middle East. The oryx has been the inspiration for many poems and stories in Saudi Arabia.

(A Closer Look, page 64)

Arts

Art in Saudi Arabia is largely dictated by Islam. Since the Qur'an forbids artists to use any form of nature in their artwork, most Saudi and Islamic art in general consists of intricate geometric and floral shapes and designs called arabesque.

Calligraphy: The Art of Fine Handwriting

Calligraphy is considered one of Saudi Arabia's highest art forms. People decorate their homes with tiles and plaques that are inscribed with beautifully written quotes from the Qur'an.

Calligraphy adorns metal work, ceramics, glass, textiles, paintings, and sculptures throughout Saudi Arabia. Fancy patterns adorn many hand-lettered Qur'ans. Many Saudi museums display collections of rare, beautifully written manuscripts. Government organizations also train future calligraphers and hold contests for these budding artists.

A Strong Tradition of Crafts

Saudi Arabia has a strong tradition of beautiful, handmade crafts. The Bedouin decorate silver jewelry with pieces of amber, coral, turquoise, or pearls. Many pieces of Bedouin jewelry are made in the shape of a hand to represent the Five Pillars of Islam. Triangular and crescent-shaped jewelry has traditionally been used to ward off the "evil eye" — a look or a stare that is meant to harm others. Weaving is also an important Saudi art form that the Bedouin have perfected.

Above: **This Bedouin woman's Islamic attire shows off her ancestors' rich tradition of colorful embroidery and large, silver accessories.**

Opposite: **Embroidering the *kiswah* (KEES-wah), or cloth that covers the holy *Kabah* (KAH-bah), with delicate gold thread requires patience and skill in Arabic calligraphy.**

Left: **The Bedouin are known for wearing layers of handcrafted rings, earrings, anklets, bracelets, pendants, and head ornaments.**

Left: King Khalid International Airport can handle up to 7.5 million passengers a year.

Architecture: Mixing the Old and the New

Ancient and modern buildings in Saudi Arabia stand together in harmony. Modern Saudi architects respect and admire traditional Islamic designs and try to create a balance between new and old styles. King Saud University and the King Khalid International Airport are two examples of how architects have successfully combined traditional Islamic and modern designs.

In the past, builders used whatever materials were at hand to create houses and buildings. Builders in Riyadh often used adobe, for example, while western Saudi Arabian architects used that area's more common stone and red brick.

Saudi Arabia's mosques are perhaps the country's greatest works of art. Exquisite minarets, or towers, accent the Grand Mosque at Mecca.

MUSEUMS IN SAUDI ARABIA

Visiting museums and historical sites is a favorite Saudi pastime. The kingdom houses several museums sponsored by the government. One of them, Riyadh's Heritage Museum, brings the history of the kingdom to life through a series of artifacts and displays. The museum features the Ethnographic Hall, which displays Saudi costumes, musical instruments, weapons, and jewelry.

Music and Dance: A Saudi Heritage

The Qur'an largely forbids public performances of music and dance, but traditional music is gaining popularity in the kingdom, especially because this art form is rooted in history.

Middle Eastern music may sound strange to Western ears because it uses different notes, rhythms, and instruments. The *oud* (OOD), a gourd-shaped stringed instrument; the *rebaba* (reh-BAH-bah), a one-stringed Bedouin instrument; and the *rigg* (REEG), a type of tambourine, give Arab music some of its unique qualities.

Saudi Arabia's national dance, the men's sword dance or *ardha* (AHR-dah), began in the Najd. In this ancient performance, sword-toting men stand shoulder to shoulder while a poet sings verses or a short song. Drummers keep the beat.

Saudi Arabia's Culture Clubs

The government of Saudi Arabia has created several cultural institutions to keep the kingdom's rich cultural heritage alive. The General Presidency of Youth Welfare (GPYW) offers folklore and art workshops to young Saudis. The GPYW also sponsors literary and drama clubs and calligraphy competitions.

Below: **Ardha, the men's sword dance, is often performed by a large group of sword-bearing men at outdoor festivals. Theater performances, such as this one, are uncommon.**

Leisure and Festivals

Social life in Saudi Arabia is largely dictated by Islamic law and revolves mostly around the family and a close circle of friends. Since it is not unusual for families to build compounds — enclosed estates that contain houses for several related families — Saudi children often grow up playing games with their cousins and siblings.

Backgammon is popular in the Middle East. This 5,000–year–old game is called *tawle* (tah-LEE) in Saudi Arabia, and the click of the dice hitting the board is a common sound in the kingdom.

Surfing the Kingdom's Web

As of 1999, Saudi Arabians have enjoyed access to the Internet. The sites that Saudis are allowed to access, however, are controlled by the government. State-of-the-art mainframe computers in Riyadh prevent Saudis from looking at sites that government officials feel do not conform to Islamic values.

Below: Until recent times, Saudis built large compounds to house extended families. The rooftops serve as terraces where families can relax in the open air.

Left: On Fridays, the Muslim holy day, many families spend time at the numerous parks found in Saudi cities.

The Great Saudi Outdoors

Saudi families enjoy relaxing together in the kingdom's many parks. Saudi Arabia boasts several national parks and preserves that protect the country's wildlife. Asir National Park is the kingdom's largest national park, covering 1.1 million acres (450,000 hectares).

Saudis enjoy hiking, camping, and picnics. Saudis like to camp in national parks as well as in the desert, following the tradition of their nomadic ancestors.

Since the Red Sea off the Saudi Arabian coast contains some of the world's most exquisite coral reefs, scuba divers, swimmers, and snorkelers eagerly explore these coastal areas. Women enjoy swimming and wading, too, but they are not permitted to wear swimsuits in public since Islamic laws say they must dress modestly. Other popular water sports in Saudi Arabia include surfing, sailing, and water skiing.

THE SOUQ

The *souq* (SOOK) is the Arabian version of a shopping mall. Virtually anything a shopper needs can be found there. However, items do not have price tags. Buyers and sellers must bargain for the best price.
(A Closer Look, page 70)

Sports in the Kingdom

Like most other people in the world, Saudi Arabians know that participating in sports is good for the body and the mind. To encourage more young people to get involved in sports such as soccer, basketball, tennis, and volleyball, the Saudis have built modern, state-of-the-art sports complexes for sporting events and exercise. Almost every town, regardless of how small, houses a stadium, sports clubs, and local recreation facilities.

In more populated areas of the kingdom, the government has built giant "sports cities," which include a high-capacity stadium, Olympic-size swimming pools, and clinics for sports medicine.

Young Saudis can pursue training in many sports, from archery to soccer, at most of the country's sports facilities. Young Saudis also can train at over twenty-two youth sports camps across the kingdom.

To make sure young people are not the only ones who remain active and healthy, many Saudi communities host local league competitions, such as "Sports for All" festivals and "Folk Games Days." Recently, more golf courses have been established in the kingdom. Saudis use bright red golf balls, which make the balls much easier to find on the sandy desert courses.

Above: **Saudi boys play an exciting game of soccer.**

Gifted Saudi athletes undergo serious training and engage in regional, national, and international competitions. Saudi Arabian athletes began competing in the Olympic Games only three decades ago, but their performance has improved each time.

Basketball in the Kingdom

Although soccer is, without a doubt, the most popular sport in Saudi Arabia, basketball is becoming a close second. Basketball was first introduced in the kingdom during the 1950s by Americans who were working in Saudi Arabia, but it took a while for Saudis to embrace the sport.

With the development of sports facilities, basketball has become one of the kingdom's more popular sports. Although most people enjoy playing basketball just for fun, Saudi Arabia also boasts a talented national basketball team, which placed first in the Gulf Championships of 1996 and the Arab Basketball Championships of 1997.

Today, more than thirty basketball club teams compete in the kingdom, boasting more than four thousand active players. Those who do not like to play enjoy cheering their favorite teams on to victory.

SOCCER

Soccer is the national sport of Saudi Arabia. Children and adults alike enjoy playing soccer in the many sports facilities and parks around the kingdom.
(A Closer Look, page 68)

Below: **Hadi Souan Somayli runs with his nation's flag after winning a silver medal in the men's 400–meter hurdles at the 2000 Olympic Games in Sydney.**

Traditional Saudi Sports

Although most Saudi youths like to pursue modern sports, traditional Saudi sports, such as camel racing and falconry, are still alive and well in the kingdom. In fact, horse and camel racing are more popular today than ever before.

Horse lovers are familiar with the sleek Arabian horse. Because of its grace, intelligence, and trainability, the Arabian horse is one of the most popular horse breeds in the world. Many Saudis enjoy watching horse races, although they are not allowed to bet on a race's outcome.

Hunting is another popular traditional sport. The saluki, a dog named after an ancient southern Arabian city, is considered by many to be the world's oldest domesticated dog. This speedy breed helps Saudi hunters, and its image adorns many pieces of ancient Middle Eastern pottery and art.

FALCONRY

In falconry, a traditional Saudi sport practiced by men, pet falcons are trained to hunt small animals. Although this sport was once popular in Europe, falconry is becoming a less common pastime even in Saudi Arabia, where falcons are raised mostly as household pets.
(*A Closer Look, page 50*)

Below: **Saudis can attend horse races, although Islamic laws forbid them to bet.**

Religious Holidays

Saudi Arabians celebrate two official Islamic holidays. During these events, all government offices, private businesses, and educational institutions remain closed.

According to the Fourth Pillar of Islam, the month of *Ramadan* (rah-mah-DAHN) is a time when all devout Muslims must abstain from eating, drinking, and having sexual relations, from sunrise to sunset. The entire family then eats one meal together at the end of the day. Women prepare nutritious foods to fortify family members for the next day.

Eid Al-Fitr (EED ahl-feetr) is the feast of the breaking of the fast. It starts on the first day of the Islamic month of *Shawal* (shah-WAHL), which follows the month of Ramadan, and usually lasts for three days. This holiday is marked by enjoying specially prepared food and giving gifts.

Right before pilgrims complete the hajj, the holy pilgrimage to Mecca, they celebrate *Eid Al-Adha* (EED ahl-ahd-HAH) along with Muslims all over the world. This celebration begins on the tenth day of the month of *Zul Hijjah* (zool HEE-jah). Traditionally, to follow the prophet Abraham's example and to show their willingness to make sacrifices to Allah, people slaughter a lamb, goat, or other animal and donate the meat to a poor family in their community.

Above: **During the feast of Eid Al-Fitr, Muslims celebrate the breaking of the fast by visiting friends and relatives and by sharing a large, festive meal with them.**

Food

Before Saudis eat, they give thanks for their meal by saying, "In the name of Allah." Once they have finished, they again express their gratitude by saying, "Thanks be to Allah." At home, Saudis usually sit on cushions on the carpeted floor around a tablecloth on which the food is placed. They wash their hands with rose-scented water both before and after the meal.

Favorite Foods

Saudi Arabians start their meals with small appetizers called *meza* (meh-ZAH). Some favorites include vegetable salads; *baba ganoush* (BAH-bah GAH-noozh), a dip made from roasted eggplant; and *kibbeh* (KEEB-beh), deep-fried balls of lamb, wheat, and spices.

Saudis use many spices in their cooking, including cinnamon, cardamom, coriander, and cumin. Some traditional dishes include

Left: These male guests in a Saudi Arabian household eat a delicious Arabian meal in the men's quarters.

Above: **Arabian bread is prepared by following a specific process outlined in Islamic law.**

mensaf (MAHN-sahf), a lamb dish; and spicy chicken with tomatoes and vegetables. *Hasaa al-gareesh* (HEE-sah ahl-gah-REESH), or wheat soup, is another special treat. This soup is made from lamb, cracked wheat, tomatoes, and a sprinkling of cinnamon. Muslims, including Saudis, are not permitted to eat pork or drink alcohol, since Islamic law forbids these items.

Diners traditionally use a flat piece of bread, called *khboz* (HOH-boes), to scoop up food, although more people these days use silverware. The Bedouin, however, use the fingers of the right hand to scoop up food from a communal bowl. Saudis always use their right hands to eat, shake hands, and touch things. The left hand is considered unclean and is never used for these purposes.

Most Saudis like to finish their meal with a sweet dessert, usually honey-laden, nut-filled pastries, such as baklava, and dates, either plain or served with sweet cream. Children and adults alike enjoy nibbling on a special candy made of sesame seeds, honey, and oil. After dessert, adults usually drink gahwa, or Arabic coffee, or sometimes small cups of very sweet tea.

Arabs have a strong tradition of hospitality and treat guests like royalty. They are generous with their portions and prepare large quantities of food to honor their guests.

A CLOSER LOOK AT SAUDI ARABIA

Saudi Arabia is a country of rich landscapes and respected traditions. The kingdom is as colorful, lively, and promising as the diverse peoples who live there. Many ancient customs thrive side by side with flourishing technologies.

Just as their ancestors did for many years before them, the Bedouin still live off the land in tents in the desert. In cities, such as Jiddah and Riyadh, Saudis enjoy the most modern conveniences, including cell phones and the Internet, while maintaining a proud connection with their history and culture.

Saudi Arabia obtains great wealth from the huge deposits of oil that lie beneath the desert, and the citizens work hard to maintain this important industry. Still, they manage to find time for relaxation by participating in camel races and falconry. Like most people, Saudis also love to shop, and they bargain heartily in the country's many souqs.

The kingdom's national religion, Islam, permeates every aspect of life. Each year, many pilgrims visit Mecca and Medina, the religion's holiest cities.

Opposite: Saudi boys, dressed in typical Saudi attire, enjoy a game of soccer, the kingdom's most popular sport.

Left: A Saudi family stops to buy soft drinks from a vending machine during a holiday outing.

The Bedouin

The life of the Bedouin — desert nomads who roam Saudi Arabia and the surrounding Middle East — has changed little since the prophet Muhammad's time in the 600s. Just as they did then, most Bedouin today live in camps in the vast desert. There, they reside in tents woven from goat or camel hair. Once a year, the women weave new tent strips on portable looms and make any needed repairs to the tent. Inside, curtains separate the men's and women's quarters.

The Bedouin typically raise goats, sheep, donkeys, or camels. Although some of these nomads now traverse the dunes in four-wheel drive vehicles, many still use camels to navigate the sands. Typically, a Bedouin family will stay in one spot for about two months, until the animals have eaten most of the area's grass and plants. At that point, they gather their belongings and move on. Since the Bedouin have few possessions and pitching a tent only takes an hour, moving is easy.

Below: **The Bedouin raise their tents in many different ways according to weather conditions. Here, the tent is pitched close to the ground to keep it from being blown over by strong winds.**

Left: Bedouin women cook the family meals and take care of the tents, which includes weaving and repairing, as well as keeping the space tidy. Men tend the herds and milk the camels.

Daily Life

The Bedouin survive mainly on milk products from the animals they raise. These desert nomads drink camel's milk for breakfast and then salt any leftover milk so it will not sour under the sun. Camel's milk is very nutritious. Besides being high in calcium, the milk is high in vitamin C. The Bedouin also enjoy rice, tomatoes, and eggs. They occasionally eat fried locusts, which taste like spinach, or grind the dried insects into a flour.

Both Bedouin women and men dress modestly. Men often carry daggers but rarely use them. The women may have tattoos on their faces and decorate the palms of their hands with henna, a plant that temporarily colors the skin reddish-brown.

At night, families sing songs, accompanied by a rebaba, a one-stringed instrument, or trade stories to pass the time. Adults and children alike enjoy *finjan* (FEEN-jahn), a game that involves uncovering a stone that is hidden under one of twelve cups.

Famous for their hospitality, the Bedouin always offer a stranger food and tea. They never turn a traveler away, with the understanding that, in the harsh desert environment, they might someday need the favor returned.

Below: Bedouin jewelry, such as these bracelets, is famous for its large, bold designs crafted in silver.

The Camel

Saudis first domesticated camels about four thousand years ago. Their remarkable ability to survive in the harsh desert terrain earned them the nickname the "ships of the desert." Camels are such an important part of Saudi culture that the kingdom's new twelve-volume *Encyclopedia of Folklore of the Kingdom of Saudi Arabia* includes an entire 547-page book on camels!

The camel's body is ideally suited to Saudi Arabia's dry climate. Saudi Arabian dromedaries have one hump in which they store vast quantities of fat, and, when food is scarce, they live off these fat reserves. Thanks to their two-toed, padded feet, camels do not sink in the desert sands. Their long eyelashes protect their eyes from the sun and stinging sandstorms. Camels are about 7 feet (2 m) tall at the shoulder.

Left: **Camels are indispensable to desert dwellers. The Bedouin prefer female camels to male camels because females are easier to train and can provide milk for a year and a half after giving birth.**

The King's Cup Camel Race

Despite their awkward appearance, camels are speedy creatures. They can walk at a rate of almost 10 miles (16 km) per hour. Each year, more than two thousand camels and riders compete in the King's Cup Camel Race in the desert near Riyadh's airport. The demanding 12-mile (19-km) race takes about two hours to finish, and top finishers receive prize money. To improve their chances of winning, the young male riders often attach themselves to the saddle with Velcro to make sure they do not fall off the camel during the bumpy ride! The King's Cup is not the only camel race in the kingdom. In fact, camel races are held in Riyadh every Monday during winter.

Although most urban Saudis today own cars, camels still remain the desert dwellers' most efficient and least expensive means of transportation. Times are changing, however. These days, the Bedouin often transport their camels to races in the back of four-wheel-drive vehicles. After all the years of carrying passengers and cargo, it is time the camels get a ride!

Above: Camel races are popular throughout Saudi Arabia, and riders are trained to compete at a young age.

The Date Palm

The date palm is so important to Saudi Arabia that it is part of the kingdom's national emblem — a date palm above two crossed swords.

For thousands of years, the fruit of the date palm has been an important part of the Saudi Arabian diet, and, next to oil, dates are Saudi Arabia's most important natural resource. Over one million date palms thrive in the kingdom's hot, dry weather. A single date palm tree can produce as much as 600 pounds (272 kilograms) of the sweet fruit in just one year. Saudi Arabia grows 600 varieties of dates, which add up to about 60 percent of all the dates produced in the world. Many people believe the world's tastiest dates come from Medina.

The date is a drupe, or a fruit whose seed is hidden inside a hard pit. Other drupes include plums and peaches.

Below: **The date industry is second only to the oil industry in Saudi Arabia.**

Feeding a Sweet Tooth

Many Saudis have a real sweet tooth. Dry dates, cured by the hot sun while they hang on the tree, are enjoyed throughout Saudi Arabia. People sometimes soften them with milk or eat them with a thick cheese that is similar to cottage or ricotta cheese.

Saudi women make sweetmeats, a type of candy, from dates. Sweetmeats do not spoil easily and can be stored for a long time. *Al-batheeth* (ahl-bah-TEETH) is a kind of sweetmeat. To make this treat, the dates are cooked with flour and butter and are seasoned with ginger and cardamom, a sweet, pungent spice. They are then rolled into balls for storing. These sweet ovals are eaten with a sprinkling of sugar. Ever resourceful, the Saudis often save the date molasses left over from this recipe to flavor bread; *muhammar* (mah-HAHM-ahr), or sweet rice; and other dishes.

An Important Resource

Versatile date palms serve as an important source of wood for making buildings. They also provide much-needed shade and serve as elegant landscape trees. The feathery palm fronds are used to make ropes, mats, and baskets.

Above: **Dates are an essential part of Saudi Arabian meals. They are eaten as snacks and used to sweeten coffee and tea.**

Falconry

Some Arabian men indulge in the ancient sport of falconry, which involves training their pet falcons to hunt for small animals. As is the case with many other Saudi traditions, falconry probably started with the Bedouin. According to legend, the Bedouin observed the falcon's extraordinary hunting talents and eventually captured some birds and taught them to hunt small game in the desert. Some sources say this sport dates back to 2000 B.C.

Saudi Arabia and the Middle East are not the only places where people practice this sport. Falconry also became very popular with the European nobility between the tenth and seventeenth centuries, but fell out of favor when guns were introduced. After World War I, falconry once again became the rage in Great Britain and Europe, probably due to the influence of Lawrence of Arabia and his interest in Arab culture.

There are about sixty different species in the falcon family. Their sharp, hooked claws, stout necks, and sharp bills help them attack their prey.

Below: Although falconry as a hunting sport is becoming less common in Saudi Arabia, Saudi men still enjoy teaching their birds clever tricks.

An expert falconer can teach a falcon to hunt in less than three weeks. Falcons usually hunt rabbits and other birds. The falcon sits, or perches, on its owner's forearm. To protect his hand and arm from the bird's sharp claws, the falconer wears a thick glove. He keeps his pet's head covered with a tiny hood to make sure the bird stays calm until the hunt begins. Once the falconer spots his prey, he quickly removes the falcon's hood, and, with a heavy jerk of his forearm, lets the bird fly after the unlucky creature. Once the falcon catches its prey, it stays with the prey until the owner arrives. The owner then gives the falcon a special treat as a reward — usually a tasty morsel of raw meat. He then puts the hood back on the bird to keep it calm.

Today, few men in the country actually hunt, even with falcons. Still, they enjoy teaching their pets different commands and developing strong friendships with their birds.

FALCON FEATURES

Falcons are aerial acrobats. These birds can fly quickly and perform dazzling maneuvers as they soar through the air. Their excellent eyesight contributes to their hunting prowess. In the wild, falcons live alone or in pairs, a trait that makes them well-suited to life with humans, since falcons do not depend on each other to survive. Although falcons can live as long as fifteen years, their hunting "careers" usually take place during the first five years of their lives, since their senses are sharpest during this time.

Gahwa

Making, serving, and drinking gahwa, or Saudi Arabian coffee, is an ancient tradition that began with the Bedouin. Supposedly, a Saudi goat herder named Khalid started this famous ritual about twelve centuries ago. Khalid noticed that, while the hot sun made him sleepy and sluggish, his goats remained full of energy all afternoon. When he saw his goats eating beans that grew on a certain tree, Khalid decided to give them a try. The herder ground and boiled these beans and created a Saudi tradition — afternoon coffee — that exists to this day.

The gahwa ceremony begins when the host places four coffee pots, or *della* (DEH-lah), by an open fire. He then dumps the coffee beans into a *mahmasa* (MAH-hah-mah-sah), or iron pan, and roasts the beans above the flames. Once the beans are roasted and cooled, he mashes them with a pestle, or *mahbash* (MAH-bahsh).

THE WATER PIPE

In Saudi Arabia, many men unwind by smoking a water pipe — a large, glass and brass, lamp-like pipe (*above*). A dish on top holds sweet tobacco and charcoal, while the hot water in the glass portion makes the steam that the men smoke through a tube. Saudis often indulge in water pipes in all-male cafés, while they share the day's news and drink a cup of gahwa.

Left: A Bedouin man uses a mahmasa — an iron pan with a long handle — to roast coffee beans over an outdoor fire. Men are usually in charge of preparing and pouring the gahwa.

The largest della holds coffee grounds from previous days, so the host pours water and the freshly ground coffee into the second largest pot, which he then boils over the flame. While the coffee brews, the host mashes cardamom seeds and perhaps a bit of saffron with the mahbash. He then puts this aromatic mixture into the third della, fills this della with the coffee from the second della and boils the coffee again.

At last, the host pours the delicious gahwa into the fourth and smallest pot to serve to his thirsty guests. The host always serves his guests, and Saudi etiquette dictates a specific order in which he must serve the coffee. The main guest receives his gahwa first. If there is any doubt about who is the main guest, the oldest person wins this honor.

Although the cups are only half filled, guests may request as many refills as they wish. To be polite, a guest must never refuse the first cup of coffee and should accept only an odd number of cups — one, three, or five. To let his host know that he has had enough, the guest shakes the empty cup from side to side. Fresh dates, not sugar, sweeten the gahwa.

Above: **Elegant della, or Arabian coffee pots, come in different sizes and serve different purposes in the making of gahwa.**

The Hajj Pilgrimage

All Muslims bow toward the Saudi city of Mecca when they say their daily prayers. Mecca is Islam's most sacred city and the site of an important Muslim religious pilgrimage called the hajj. One of the Five Pillars of Islam dictates that every devout Muslim try to visit Mecca at least once in his or her lifetime. The hajj takes place from the eighth day through the eleventh day of Zul Hijjah, the twelfth month of the Muslim lunar calendar.

Muslims arrive in Mecca from all over the world on foot; by horse, camel, and donkey; and by bus, train, ship, and airplane. All pilgrims, rich or poor, dress in the same white clothing to perform the rituals. White represents the state of purity they seek. No one is allowed in the sacred area until he or she dons these special clothes. Men wear a two-piece white robe that leaves the right arm uncovered. Women wear long white robes that cover their entire bodies. Although most cover their faces with a veil, women may make the hajj unveiled.

Left: **Muslim pilgrims from all over the world gather around the holy Kabah in the Grand Mosque at Mecca.**

Following an Ancient Path

Throughout the hajj, the pilgrims fervently express their devotion to Allah by saying *labbayk* (lah-bah-YEEK), or "I am here." At Mecca, the pilgrims enter the Grand Mosque that they believe Abraham founded. They then circle the Kabah seven times. The Kabah contains the stone Muslims believe is a part of Abraham's original temple. As a symbol of their devotion, they try to touch or kiss the stone, which is believed to absorb sins.

Following Muhammad's example, on the eighth day of Zul Hijjah, pilgrims spend the night praying in the tent city of Mina. The next day, facing Mecca, they pray from sunrise to sunset on Mount Arafat. Once they leave Arafat, the pilgrims believe they have washed away their sins. Later, they throw pebbles at three pillars in Mina that represent evil.

On the tenth day of Zul Hijjah, imitating Abraham's sacrifice, each pilgrim sacrifices a goat or sheep and donates the meat to the poor. At the same time, Muslims around the world remember Abraham during this special feast called Eid Al-Adha. Before leaving Mecca, the pilgrims must pray at the Kabah one more time. Many pilgrims end their hajj by visiting Medina.

Above: Pilgrims pray at Mount Arafat from sunrise to sunset to wash away their sins during a ritual of the hajj.

Below: The attire for the hajj has remained the same throughout the ages, as shown in this ancient print.

Islam in Saudi Arabia

In A.D. 570, Muhammad was born to a poor family in Mecca. Even as a child, he always loved to pray. Once, while he was meditating in a cave, the angel Gabriel gave him a message from Allah, or God, which said that young Muhammad was Allah's prophet. He then devoted his life to preaching Islam.

Muhammad's followers compiled his teachings in the holy Qur'an, the religion's sacred book. Since his death in 632, Islam has spread to neighboring nations and other countries all over the world. Today, there are about one billion followers of Islam, called Muslims, in the world. *Islam* means "submission" in Arabic.

Islam is the kingdom's official religion, and the practice of any other religion in Saudi Arabia is not allowed. Muslims from all over the world consider the kingdom a sort of homeland. When Muslims pray, they face in the direction of Mecca, and, each year, thousands of faithful pilgrims flock to the holy cities of Mecca and Medina.

Below: **The Islamic faith was born in Saudi Arabia, but today, the religion has grown to include people of all races and nationalities.**

56

Above: **Saudi men pray before the start of a horse race.**

The Five Pillars of Islam

All Muslims must obey the following five basic principles that rule their daily lives.

First, Muslims must believe and openly declare the *shahada* (shee-HAH-daht), which states, "There is no god but Allah and Muhammad is His Prophet." Second, all Muslims must perform prayers, or *salah* (sah-LAH), five times each day facing Mecca. *Zakat* (zah-KAHT), the third pillar, or principle, states that Muslims must donate a portion of their possessions to the community, especially to its poorest members. During Ramadan, the ninth month of the Islamic calendar, Muslims must perform *sawm* (SOWM), or fasting. They must not eat, drink, or have sexual relations between sunrise and sunset. Last, Muslims must try to go on the hajj pilgrimage to Saudi Arabia's holy city of Mecca at least once during their lives.

Sunnis and Shiites

Most Saudis are Sunni Muslims. A small group of Shiite Muslims lives on the kingdom's east coast. The major difference between the two groups is the way they interpret Muhammad's successors. Also, unlike Sunnis, Shiites worship the prophets.

Jiddah

Jiddah began almost 2,500 years ago as a remote Red Sea fishing village. Today, however, it is a bustling metropolis. The city has always been called the "Bride of the Sea." When Egypt's Suez Canal (the canal that links the Red Sea with the Mediterranean Sea) opened in 1869, Jiddah was turned into a major trading city.

During the oil boom in the 1970s, Jiddah prospered even more and became Saudi Arabia's main seaport. Today, several oil refineries operate in the city, and Jiddah's waterfront workers ship oil to places all over the world. Almost two million people live in the metropolis, making Jiddah the largest city in the kingdom's western region.

In the 1920s, only one tree grew within the city's old walls. Today, thanks to an efficient watering system, grass, trees, and flowers make Jiddah a colorful place to live. This bounty is due, in part, to a large desalination plant. This plant removes the salt from about five million gallons of Red Sea water each day, providing Saudis with water for drinking, bathing, washing, and gardening.

Below: **The Humane Heritage Museum in Jiddah is a colorful and charming re-creation of the city as it was in the past.**

Above: **Facing the Red Sea, Jiddah's cityscape is a blend of modern and traditional styles.**

The Old Meets the New

Even though Jiddah is not as politically important as Saudi Arabia's capital, Riyadh, its residents still feel it is the country's most charming place to live. Both natives and foreign workers enjoy the city's many beautiful restaurants, parks, sculptures, hotels, fountains, and gardens located in the Corniche, a recreation area along the beach. At night, Jiddah's twinkling skyline is reflected in the waters of the Red Sea.

Although the town has many modern facilities, Jiddah proudly retains its ancient charm. The buildings in the Old City are crafted out of coral from the Red Sea's coral reefs.

Pilgrims' Rest Stop

Many pilgrims on their way to Mecca enter the country through the city's King Abdul Aziz International Airport. Its Hajj Terminal is the largest covered space in the world. The terminal's tentlike design mimics the shape of the tents of the devout Muslims who make the pilgrimage. The facility was designed to accommodate these large numbers of visitors, and staff members are trained to answer their questions and help them. Over the years, many foreign Muslims who made the hajj decided to stay in Saudi Arabia and settled in Jiddah. The city's residents have roots in many places, including Africa, Iran, India, and Southeast Asia.

OLD CHARM

Although Jiddah is a modern city in every sense — tall buildings and high-tech factories line its streets — Jiddah proudly retains its ancient charm. Small hotels that once gave shelter to pilgrims and merchants still line the mazelike ancient streets, along with old-world shops that sell spices, meats, perfumes, fruits, and vegetables. Wooden balconies, remnants of the Ottoman Turks' influence, adorn some buildings.

Lawrence of Arabia

Thomas Edward Lawrence was born in Wales in 1888. Even as a boy, Lawrence was fascinated by ancient civilizations. While he attended Oxford University, Lawrence traveled to Palestine and Syria to do research for a project on Crusader castles. These castles were built by Christian soldiers during the Crusades, a series of wars that took place between European Christians and Muslims, from the eleventh to the thirteenth centuries.

After earning a degree in archaeology, Lawrence worked on the British Museum's excavation of the ancient city of Carchemish in present-day Turkey. While there, Lawrence practiced his Arabic and learned more about Middle Eastern culture.

Left: **T. E. Lawrence, the British archaeologist and soldier immortalized as "Lawrence of Arabia," jotted down his adventures in the Middle East in his book** *Seven Pillars of Wisdom.*

The Arab's Secret Weapon

Lawrence was among the first Westerners to fight for Arab nationhood, and he became known as "Amir Dynamite" among the Arabs.

The Ottoman Turks had occupied the Middle East since the 1600s, and the Arabs wanted to drive them and their German allies from the area. In 1916, during World War I, Arabs in Mecca attacked the Turks. The Ottomans quickly sent more soldiers and supplies into Medina by way of the Hijaz Railroad. The Arab cause seemed to be doomed.

By this time, however, the Arabs had acquired their own secret weapon. The British had offered the Arabs the services of T. E. Lawrence. Lawrence was a superb tactician and leader. He taught the Arabs guerrilla warfare techniques, which they used against their country's invaders.

Below: T. E. Lawrence led Bedouin troops across the Arabian desert in successful campaigns against the Ottoman Turks.

In 1917, Lawrence and about thirty Bedouin made their way through the Hijaz Mountains, in northwestern Saudi Arabia, to capture Aqaba, now a city in Jordan, at the mouth of the Red Sea. Lawrence and his forces surprised the Turks, who had expected them to arrive by sea, and captured Aqaba. Lawrence's small successes paved the way for the Allied victory in the Middle East.

Lawrence continued to serve in the British forces in the Middle East until his retirement in 1935 at the age of forty-six. He died on May 19, 1935, after a motorcycle accident.

Oil

In the 1930s, geologists discovered huge pools of petroleum, or crude oil, beneath the soil in Saudi Arabia. Due to these vast oil deposits, much of the world's petroleum products come from the kingdom. This thick, black substance, nicknamed "black gold," burns and produces energy very efficiently. After it is purified, or refined, the oil fuels countless machines that we use every day, including cars, airplanes, and lawn mowers.

Through a combination of good fortune in geography and savvy business skills, oil has made Saudi Arabia a wealthy nation. The government keeps a tight grip on the industry on which the nation's economy is based. Saudi law states that all oil companies in the nation must be owned by the Saudi government or by Saudi citizens. The biggest Saudi oil company is Aramco.

While many people in the world grumble about the high cost of gasoline, Saudis are not among them. The cost of gas in Saudi Arabia is the lowest in the world — only about 10 cents per gallon!

Below: **This oil storage facility is located off the coast of Yanbu Al-Bahr. Saudi Arabia's profitable oil industry has turned the small fishing town into a world-class city.**

Oil accounts for 90 percent of the Saudi economy. About half the country's refined petroleum is used for gas. The other half is used to make dyes, paint, ink, plastics, and chemicals. Many countries purchase oil from Saudi Arabia. Its biggest customers include the United States, Japan, Singapore, and South Korea.

Once the oil is gathered, a huge network of pipelines pumps it from the drilling sites in eastern Saudi Arabia to refineries in the west, where it is purified. Transporting crude oil along this pipeline is faster and less expensive than shipping it by sea, and the pipeline has saved the oil industry both time and money.

Although the oil industry promotes a healthy economy in the kingdom, oil production endangers the environment. About 250,000 gallons (946,000 liters) of oil are accidentally spilled into the Persian Gulf each year, killing wildlife and polluting the waters. One of the worst oil spills occurred during the Persian Gulf War, when an oil storage tank exploded in the neighboring country of Kuwait. The slick polluted over 267 miles (430 km) of Saudi coastline and destroyed about 300,000 seabirds and even more marine creatures. Today, the kingdom is working hard to control pollution and preserve the environment.

Below: A complex and efficient system of pipework, like this one in Yanbu Al-Bahr, ensures the swift and smooth transportation of oil from coast to coast.

The Oryx

The Myth of the Unicorn

When you look at the Arabian oryx from the side and from a distance, its two spiraling horns seem to melt into one. This antelopelike creature probably inspired the myth of the unicorn — the legendary single-horned, horselike creature that is the subject of many great works of art. According to Guillaume of Normandy's *Le Bestiaire Divin*, the unicorn could not be captured unless it laid its head on the lap of an innocent girl. Only then would the beast be soothed and grow calm enough to be captured.

Snowy white, with a few prominent black markings dotting its face, the graceful oryx stands about 40 inches (1 m) tall. The elegant gray horns extend almost 20 inches (50 cm), and the legs are mostly black with white, socklike bands. Female oryx have slightly longer but thinner horns than males. These horns adorn the oryx's head and also protect it from predators. Oryx have been known to kill lions and jackals with their horns.

Above: **The strikingly graceful Arabian oryx has inspired countless legends since antiquity.**

Inspiring Poets

Arabian poets also wrote about the oryx's graceful movements and compared the delicate animal to a beautiful woman. Like the oryx, the Bedouin navigated the endless desert sands, and they admired the animal's ability to thrive in such a harsh environment. These nomads felt that if a hunter captured an oryx, he would acquire the strength, courage, and endurance of the animal. Not surprisingly, the Bedouin believed the prized meat of the oryx possessed special healing powers.

A Desert Survivor

The Bedouin were right about the oryx's ability to survive. Like camels, this animal needs little water, and, in some rare cases, it can survive for years without drinking. Instead, the oryx gathers moisture by licking dew from plants and by extracting liquid from the vegetation it consumes, which includes desert grass, broomrape, and desert gourds. During the rare periods of rain in the desert, the oryx "sniffs out" precious liquid from great distances, and it has no trouble locating fresh puddles of water.

UNICORN HISTORY

The unicorn's history goes as far back as the fifth century B.C., when several Greek historians wrote about an exotic type of mule. The unicorn was portrayed in Greek accounts as being the size of a horse and as having a horse's head, a deer's legs, a lion's tail, and a goat's beard. The white unicorn was also described as having blue eyes and a red head.

A Creature in Danger

The oryx once loped daintily across the entire Arabian peninsula, but too much hunting and development has threatened the herds. By 1972, the oryx was near extinction. Only a few small groups survived by fleeing to the Rub Al-Khali, or Empty Quarter, far away from the threats of zealous hunters and human communities.

Some concerned Saudi citizens understood the seriousness of the problem and put conservation efforts into motion by telling the late King Khalid about the animal's plight. The king made certain the oryx was reintroduced into the Arabian environment.

Now protected from hunters, the oryx's numbers are on the rise. They can still be spotted on the dunes, seeming to glide across the desert landscape. Several zoos, including the San Diego Zoo in the United States, have been trying to reintroduce oryx that were born in captivity to their natural Saudi habitat. If all goes well, the oryx will be able to survive one of its greatest challenges — the progress of modern society.

Below: **The mythical unicorn was the subject of numerous works of art in medieval Europe.**

Riyadh

Located in the eastern central part of the Arabian Peninsula and covering an area of more than 600 square miles (1,554 sq km), Riyadh started out as a tiny village lined with crude buildings made of sun-baked bricks. The village was, more or less, an oasis in the desert. Today, Riyadh has grown into one of the Middle East's most important cities and is the capital of Saudi Arabia.

Humble Beginnings

The founder of Saudi Arabia, Ibn Saud, named Riyadh the capital in 1932, but the city grew slowly. By the 1940s, only about 50,000 people lived in the city.

In the 1970s, the booming oil business made many Saudis wealthy. They used the newly earned money to modernize their capital city. They created new buildings and houses, developed modern schools and facilities, and introduced new technology to the city. As a result, more people flocked to Riyadh to take advantage of this progress.

Today, Riyadh is the largest city in Saudi Arabia, and about 3.3 million people call Riyadh home. Modern apartment complexes have replaced the mud houses, while playgrounds and parks are reminiscent of the lush oasis.

Below: **Before its emergence as the capital of the Kingdom of Saudi Arabia, Riyadh's buildings, such as this old fort, were made mainly out of coarse mud bricks.**

A Place to Learn and Work

Since Riyadh is the political center of the country, the embassies of about ninety nations around the world are located in a special neighborhood within the capital.

Riyadh is also an educational center and is home to several universities, including the Islamic University of Imam Muhammad Ibn Saud, the King Abdul Aziz Military Academy, and King Saud University. All three were built in the 1950s. Nearly 32,000 students from around the globe study at King Saud University, including more than 5,000 women.

Children enjoy visiting the zoo. Built in 1987, the new Riyadh Zoo is home to 1,400 animals, including the endangered houbara bustard, the griffon vulture, and the sand cat.

Riyadh is also a transportation hub. People from foreign countries enter the kingdom by landing at King Khalid International Airport. It is the largest airport in the world, covering about 87 square miles (225 square km).

Everyday life in Riyadh was interrupted in 1991 during the Persian Gulf War, when neighboring Iraq fired many missiles into the city. Fortunately, the missiles did not cause much damage.

Today, Riyadh is undoubtedly a brilliant Saudi Arabian jewel. However, in case the Saudis forget their capital's humble beginnings, the primitive mud fort that Ibn Saud captured still stands as a well-preserved tourist attraction in the city center.

Above: **The building of the Ministry of the Interior is one of Riyadh's most famous landmarks. Its design is modern and sleek, yet the building is topped by an unmistakably Arab-style dome.**

Soccer

Soccer is the sport of choice for many Saudi Arabians, and they heartily cheer their teams on to victory. In fact, soccer is the kingdom's national sport. One of King Fahd's sons serves as the president of the Saudi Football Federation, while another son serves as vice president .

Soccer is more than just a spectator sport in the kingdom. Children and adults alike enjoy playing this sport in parks, stadiums, and courtyards.

The Saudi National Team

Saudis are passionate about their national team. During matches, cafés are filled with men who are not shy about shrieking, cheering, and shouting at televisions transmitting the match.

The year 1984 was quite memorable for Saudi soccer fans. The Saudi team upset several tough opponents to qualify for its first appearance in the finals of the 1984 Olympic soccer competition in Los Angeles. Later that year, the Saudis captured the Asian Games Gold Cup. In 2002, the Saudi team played impressively to qualify for the World Cup but were defeated by Ireland in the first round.

Left: **The Saudi soccer delegation holds onto the Arab Cup trophy after clinching the title in a match against Qatar, held in Doha, Qatar, in 1998.**

A Spectacular Goal

Through hard work and determination, the Saudi team continues to improve. In 1993, the Saudis emerged in first place in the Asian Division to represent the continent at the 1994 World Cup finals in the United States.

In fact, one amazing Saudi goal made during the finals has become a national, and even international, legend. *World Soccer* magazine called it "probably the finest solo goal the World Cup finals have ever seen."

During a match against Belgium, played in 110° F (43° C) heat at RFK Stadium in Washington, D.C., one of the team's best players, Saeed Al-Owairan, took control of the ball. He gracefully sped across the field, skillfully avoiding five Belgian players. He finally shot the ball like a cannon past their goalkeeper, bringing his team a 1-0 victory. For his efforts, King Fahd rewarded Al-Owairan with a fancy sports car.

In the kingdom, Islam rules even soccer. Al-Owairan was sent to prison a few months after the World Cup victory. The soccer star was suspended from playing soccer for two years for violating several Islamic rules, including drinking alcohol. Today, Al-Owairan is back on the field.

Below: **Al-Owairan is Saudi Arabia's greatest soccer star.**

The Souq

The souq, or bazaar, is an important part of daily life in Saudi Arabia. Shoppers can find virtually anything they need or want in these vast marketplaces. Families often shop in the souqs together.

Many souqs are housed in ancient buildings that are made from a type of cement. They are often decorated with tiles and usually have vaulted, or arched, ceilings. Some souqs are outdoors. Merchants in the souqs sell a variety of goods, from spices, religious items, and clothing to carpets, jewelry, and pottery. Often, similar businesses are located in one area. Spice merchants might line one of the souq's narrow streets, while jewelers might keep shop in a different area.

As shoppers stroll by, vendors may call to them, enticing them to look in the booths. Vendors also sometimes hold up merchandise and yell out prices. On occasion, a vendor may offer a shopper a cup of coffee or tea.

A REST STOP

Thirsty shoppers often stop for tea in one of the countless cafés that dot the souqs. Shoppers who do not want to sit down in a café can buy tea or juice from the numerous vendors who roam the souqs. Many vendors carry tea and other beverages in elaborately decorated containers strapped to their backs. These vendors usually announce their presence by clinking two glasses together with their fingers, like cymbals.

Left: These merchants are selling gutras in a modern Saudi souq.

70

Bargaining: A Middle Eastern Art

In the Middle East, merchandise for sale does not have marked prices, as is the custom in the West. Instead, shoppers and merchants "bargain," or haggle, until they agree on a price. This ritual involves a bit of drama and showmanship, but the exchange is always friendly.

Traditionally, the merchant starts by stating a price for an item — a coffee pot, for example — that is much higher than the actual worth of the item. The buyer usually responds by stating a price that is much lower than the worth of the item. After a bit of animated debate and discussion, the two parties usually meet somewhere in the middle. If the two do not agree on a price, the merchant is under no obligation to sell, nor is the buyer under any obligation to make a purchase. Since Arabs are generally a people-loving society, this ritual is another form of social interaction and cooperation.

Above: **Saudis walk through one of the many souqs found in the kingdom. The streets of some outdoor souqs have been roofed to protect shoppers from the blazing Arabian sun. Most souqs in Saudi Arabia stay open until 10 p.m.**

Women in Saudi Arabia

The role of Saudi women is much different from that of Western women. A Saudi woman's role is defined largely by the Saudi Arabian interpretation of Islamic law.

Women in the kingdom must keep covered so they do not tempt men with their beauty. They hide their hair, arms, and legs with a long, black cloak called an abayah. Saudi Arabian women, however, still have an interest in fashion. Underneath the abayah, a Saudi woman might wear the latest designer fashions, gold jewelry, or jeans.

A Saudi woman's primary role is to serve as a good wife and mother. This is a full-time job, especially considering the fact that most Saudi women have about six children. A Saudi woman must follow many other rules. She must not speak to men or sit beside them unless they are members of her family. At home, women live, for the most part, in separate rooms from men.

SAUDI ARABIAN BUSINESSWOMEN

From its early history through present times, the Kingdom of Saudi Arabia has been home to many successful businesswomen. Khadijah, prophet Muhammad's wife, was a prominent businesswoman in Mecca. More recently, Mayan Kurdi, a Saudi woman with a master's degree in business administration, set up NetPeople, a company that provides Internet services to businesses and individuals. The company employs only women.

Left: An increase in educational opportunities has allowed many Saudi women to hold professional jobs in the private and public sectors.

A Separate World

A sharp division exists between men and women in Saudi Arabia. Boys and girls are kept apart from an early age — in the classroom as well as in places of business.

In the 1980s, only 55 percent of girls in Saudi Arabia went to elementary school and only 23 percent went on to high school. Today, these numbers are on the rise. The five thousand women who are studying at Riyadh's King Saud University reflect this change in attitude. Still, at the university, women may not attend a lecture that a male professor or speaker delivers, although she may watch it on closed-circuit television.

Since Islam dictates that women should be financially independent, Saudi women are able to run their own businesses and can inherit and own property. However, women must do their banking at separate women's branches.

Women are not allowed to drive. If a Saudi woman wants to go out, her husband or a male relative must go with her. If she must go out alone, a driver transports her. Men and women even attend separate wedding celebrations.

In their unique way, Saudi women contribute a great deal to life and culture in the kingdom.

Above: Saudi women are required by Islamic law to wear the long, black abayah when they go out in public.

RELATIONS WITH NORTH AMERICA

Historically, Saudi Arabia has enjoyed mostly good relations with the United States. Although the terrorist attacks of September 11, 2001 have strained relations between the countries, their similarities and spirit of cooperation serve to strengthen the strong friendship between the two nations.

The United States is a melting pot of many different cultures, races, and religions. At the same time, Muslims of every culture, race, and nationality come to Mecca in Saudi Arabia to make the hajj, or religious pilgrimage. These pilgrims include the many Muslims who live in the United States. Both countries are, in a sense, homelands for diverse groups of people, and both are committed to building sound economies.

Opposite: Muslim American women pray at Mount Arafat during the hajj pilgrimage.

Below: U.S. president Bill Clinton received a medal from King Fahd during a visit to the kingdom in 1994.

Early Days

The friendship between Saudi Arabia and the United States began in the early 1900s. United States president Woodrow Wilson's call for self-determination for nations after World War I impressed King Ibn Saud greatly. Under the policy of self-determination, groups of people would have the right to form their own home states and to choose their own governments.

During World War II, the ties between Saudi Arabia and the United States were further strengthened when King Ibn Saud and President Franklin D. Roosevelt met on board the U.S.S. *Quincy* in the Suez Canal and discussed the worsening plight of the Jewish people in Europe, as well as other international affairs.

King Saud Visits the United States

In 1957, King Saud Bin Abdul Aziz became the first Saudi ruler to visit the United States. Since then, many more meetings have occurred between Saudi and U.S. leaders. King Faisal met with President Lyndon Johnson in 1965 and then with President Richard Nixon in 1971. King Khalid met with President Jimmy Carter in Washington, D.C., in 1977 and in Riyadh in 1978. These meetings have served both as forums for discussion and gestures of friendship and goodwill.

SAUDI ARABIA AND CANADA

Although relations between Saudi Arabia and Canada do not go as far back as the kingdom's relations with the United States, Saudi-Canadian relations have become stronger in the last few years. For instance, the Saudi-Canadian Joint Economic Commission met in Riyadh in 1999 to discuss economic issues between the two nations. A memorandum signed at the end of the meeting reaffirmed the two countries' desire to promote investment in the form of joint ventures between Saudi and Canadian companies.

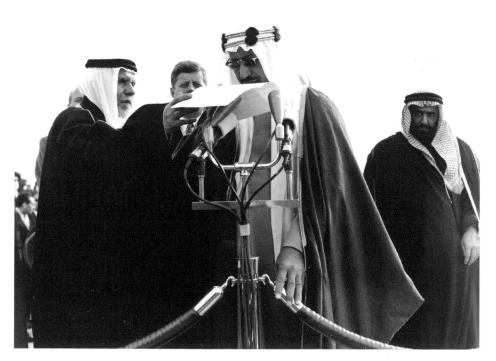

Left: King Saud gives a speech during a state visit to the United States in 1962. President John F. Kennedy stands in the background.

Above: U.S. troops had to obey Islamic laws during their stay in the kingdom in the 1991 Persian Gulf War.

The Persian Gulf War: Kuwait Invaded

In 1990, the president of Iraq, Saddam Hussein, ordered his army to invade Saudi Arabia's neighbor, the tiny, oil-rich country of Kuwait. Hussein explained the invasion by stating that, until the fall of the Ottoman Empire after World War I, Kuwait had been part of the Ottoman province of Basra, a province based around the city of Basra in present-day Iraq. While this history is true, Iraq's current borders were not set until after the fall of the Ottoman Empire. Additionally, Iraq had formally recognized Kuwait's independence from Iraq in 1963.

Both the United Nations and the Arab League condemned Hussein's act of aggression. At Saudi Arabia's request, a group of Western and Arab armed forces from twenty-seven countries moved into eastern Saudi Arabia, near the Kuwaiti border, to keep the kingdom safe from Iraqi troops. The United States sent more than 500,000 troops, 1,800 aircraft, and 100 ships to the Persian Gulf. The United States had not deployed so many troops overseas since the Vietnam War. The United States called this deployment of its armed forces "Operation Desert Shield." Once the troops went into combat, the endeavor was called "Operation Desert Storm." The Persian Gulf War, which took place along the Persian Gulf, started in January 1991.

THE PERSIAN GULF WAR AND THE ENVIRONMENT

The environment suffered serious damage during the Persian Gulf War. In what has been called the world's largest oil spill, about 240 million gallons (908 million liters) soiled the Gulf's waters, the coasts of Kuwait and Iran, and much of Saudi Arabia's Persian Gulf shoreline. Besides killing much of the kingdom's shellfish, fish, and birds, this spill has also damaged the Saudi fishing industry.

Social and Economic Interests

The coalition force's primary objective was to drive Iraq from Kuwait and to protect the small nation. At the same time, almost all countries involved had many of their own interests in helping Kuwait and Saudi Arabia. The United States, for example, wanted to show its allegiance to Saudi Arabia, but it also wanted to protect its oil and military interests in the Middle East. Saudi Arabia wanted to keep the invaders from entering the kingdom and from harming its citizens. The leaders of the two nations knew that holding back the Iraqi forces would benefit both countries in the long term.

Above: **Many oil fields, such as these in Kuwait, were bombed during the Persian Gulf War, causing large and extremely harmful oil spills.**

Iraq Enters Saudi Arabia

On January 29, 1991, seven hundred troops from Iraq invaded Saudi Arabia. They captured Ras Al-Khafji, a small town. Luckily, most of the people there had temporarily moved away because of the dangers the war had presented. Coalition planes then took off from oil fields in Saudi Arabia to bomb Baghdad, the capital of Iraq. With the help of Qatar's army, the Saudi and coalition forces were able to drive out the Iraqi army.

Military Allies

Because of its location, Saudi Arabia serves as a strategic military position in the Middle East. Several U.S. military bases are located in the kingdom. The United States also sells military equipment, including aircraft and weapons, to the Saudi Arabian military.

After September 11, 2001

The terrorist attacks on September 11, 2001, have led the United States and Saudi Arabia into a newly complicated relationship. Fifteen of the nineteen hijackers were Saudi citizens, and although the Saudi Arabian government supports U.S. efforts to combat terrorism, many Saudis are believed to sympathize with the cause of Osama bin Laden. Bin Laden is widely held as the leader of the al-Qaeda network, a radical rebel group the U.S. government holds responsible for the terrorist attacks in 2001.

Left: Aramco, or the Arabian American Oil Company, has a long history in the kingdom. A plaque commemorates the founding of the partnership in 1936.

The Saudi Ambassador to the United States

As a child, Prince Bandar Bin Sultan attended American schools. Bandar earned his degree in international relations and politics from Johns Hopkins University in the United States. With his keen understanding of both cultures, Bandar has helped nurture the friendly relationship between the two countries.

Above: Approximately 35,000 Americans work in the kingdom. Most are employed in the oil industry or in medical or teaching fields. Here, Americans shop for Arabian carpets.

Americans in the Kingdom

Currently, more than 35,000 Americans and their families live in Saudi Arabia. In fact, the largest U.S. civilian school system abroad is located in the kingdom. Americans work in a variety of fields in the kingdom, including health care, oil production, and education. Many members of the United States military are also stationed at bases in Saudi Arabia.

Americans who live in the kingdom must show respect for the country's unique culture, customs, and religion. Women, for example, must cover their bodies and hair when they are in public. All foreigners — whether they are Muslim or not — must show respect during the Islamic month of Ramadan by not eating in public. Foreigners, however, are not required to fast.

Saudis Visit North America

Some Saudi Arabians — mostly boys and men — attend schools in the United States. Over three thousand Saudis are currently studying in American universities. In fact, many members of the royal family have received their college educations in the United States. Compared to other nationalities, however, only a handful of Saudis live permanently in the United States. Besides settling in large urban areas, such as New York, many Arab immigrants have also moved to the state of Michigan.

American Facilities Bombed

Although the relationship between Saudi Arabia and the United States has been, for the most part, friendly, it has been strained on a few occasions even before September 11, 2001. In 1995, a bomb exploded near a Riyadh building used by the U.S. military. In 1996, the U.S. military complex in Dhahran, Saudi Arabia, was bombed, and nineteen Americans and many Saudis were killed. Although several Saudi citizens eventually confessed to the bombings in Dhahran, many people feel their actions were part of a larger anti-Western plot.

Below: **Although Saudi Arabia is a relatively safe country, terrorist attacks, such as the bombing in Dhahran, targeted at Americans have happened on a few occasions.**

The Human Rights Question

A major area of disagreement between the United States and Saudi Arabia is the issue of human rights. Many people and organizations in the United States have expressed concern about the kingdom's human rights record. The United States government, however, in an effort to maintain the strong relationship between the two countries, has not done much to publicly criticize the kingdom.

King Fahd: Cementing a Friendship

King Fahd established firm and positive ties with North America. As Crown Prince, he had met with several United States leaders many times. His first presidential meeting as king included a conference with President Ronald Reagan in 1985. In 1990, King Fahd met with President George Bush to talk about a solution to the Iraqi occupation of Kuwait, which led to the Persian Gulf War and the eventual liberation of Kuwait. King Fahd helped make Saudi Arabia-United States ties even stronger when he met with President Bill Clinton in Hafr Al-Batin in 1994 to discuss a variety of issues.

Below, left: **The late King Faisal worked hard at developing relations with Western countries. He is seen here with former U.S. president Lyndon Johnson.**

Below, right: **Known for his strong relations with the West, King Fahd walks with U.S. president Jimmy Carter in 1978.**

Crown Prince Abdullah, whose views are more anti-West than King Fahd's, has been running the country since Fahd became ill. Many North Americans and Europeans worry that his views might contribute to an increasingly strained relationship with the United States.

Above: **King Fahd has met with every one of the last five U.S. presidents since taking control of the Saudi Arabian government in the late 1970s. Here, King Fahd shakes hands with President George Bush.**

Cultural Connections

Saudi Arabia has long been considered a "closed society." For many years, the country was not open to tourists, and getting a visa to visit the kingdom was very difficult. The Saudi government wanted to make sure that the people of the kingdom did not become influenced by the customs and cultures of the West, especially in the area of religion. The government wanted to make sure the laws of Islam were obeyed.

Recently, however, Saudi Arabia has opened its doors to cultural and educational tours. A group from the Smithsonian Institution in the United States traveled to the kingdom to learn about the nation's rich heritage — its culture, art, and religion.

83

Learning about Saudi Arabia

North Americans can learn about Saudi Arabia's unique culture and customs in a variety of ways.

Cultural exhibits that allow Americans a glimpse into Saudi Arabia's heritage and culture have traveled around the United States. "Saudi Arabia: Yesterday and Today," one of the most successful of such programs, traveled to many major American cities, including Atlanta, Dallas, New York, Boston, Los Angeles, and Washington, D.C. This exhibit promoted a better understanding of the kingdom among Americans.

The Saudi Arabian Embassy in the United States has recently created a web site that gives readers extensive information about the kingdom, including Saudi history, current happenings, and even sports reports.

Some friendships go beyond borders. In 1985, the first Arab and Muslim astronaut, Saudi Prince Sultan Bin Salman Bin Abdul Aziz, traveled into space as payload specialist aboard the United States space shuttle *Discovery*.

Opposite: **Riyadh Bank, like other banks in Saudi Arabia, relies on the support of the kingdom's highly profitable oil industry.**

Below: **Saudi Arabia has tried to keep foreign influence in the kingdom to a minimum, but many well-known American products have found their way into the Saudi Arabian market.**

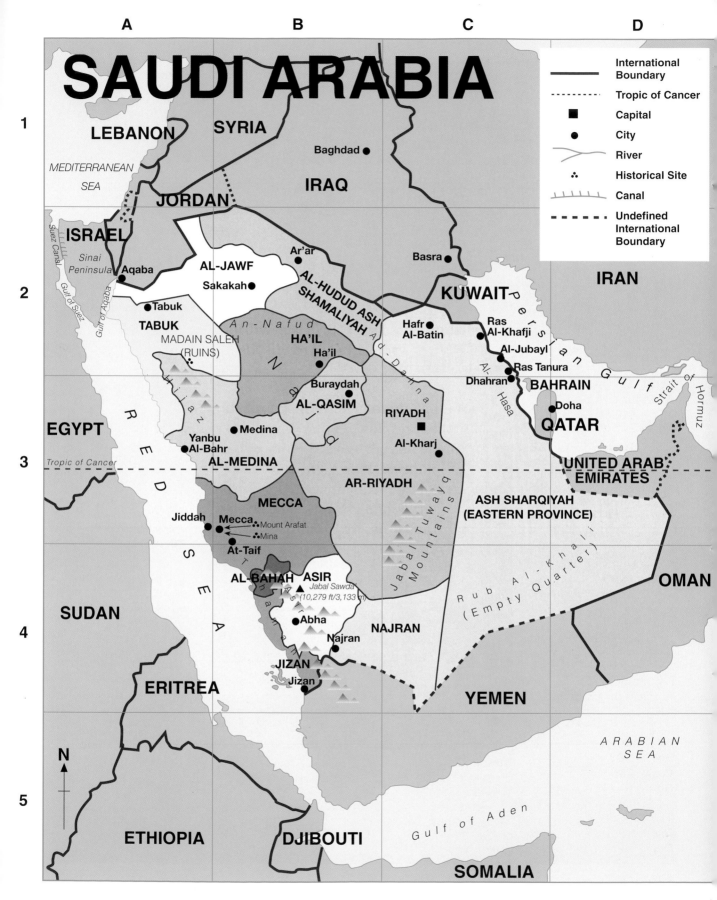

SAUDI ARABIA

International Boundary
Tropic of Cancer
■ Capital
● City
River
∴ Historical Site
Canal
Undefined International Boundary

LEBANON
SYRIA
MEDITERRANEAN SEA
JORDAN
IRAQ
Baghdad ●
ISRAEL
Suez Canal
Sinai Peninsula
Gulf of Suez
Gulf of Aqaba
Aqaba ●
● Tabuk
TABUK
MADAIN SALEH (RUINS)
An - Nafud
AL-JAWF
Sakakah ●
Ar'ar ●
AL-HUDUD ASH SHAMALIYAH
Basra ●
KUWAIT
Ras Al-Khafji
Hafr Al-Batin ●
IRAN
HA'IL
Ha'il ●
Ad-Dahna
Al-Jubayl
Ras Tanura
Dhahran ●
Persian Gulf
Strait of Hormuz
Buraydah ●
AL-QASIM
BAHRAIN
Doha ●
QATAR
EGYPT
RED SEA
Hijaz
Yanbu Al-Bahr ●
● Medina
RIYADH ■
Al-Kharj ●
Al-Hasa
AL-MEDINA
Tropic of Cancer
AR-RIYADH
ASH SHARQIYAH (EASTERN PROVINCE)
UNITED ARAB EMIRATES
MECCA
Jiddah ●
Mecca ● ∴ Mount Arafat
∴ Mina
At-Taif ●
Jabal Tuwayq Mountains
Rub Al-Khali (Empty Quarter)
OMAN
AL-BAHAH
ASIR
▲ Jabal Sawda (10,279 ft/3,133 m)
Abha ●
Najran ●
NAJRAN
SUDAN
Tihama
JIZAN
Jizan ●
YEMEN
ERITREA
ETHIOPIA
DJIBOUTI
Gulf of Aden
ARABIAN SEA
SOMALIA

N

Above: A Saudi farmer and his children work the land in Najran.

Abha B4
Ad-Dahna (desert)
     B2–C3
Al-Bahah B4
Al-Hasa (region) C2–C3
Al-Hudud ash
     Shamaliyah A2–B2
Al-Jawf A2–B2
Al-Jubayl C2
Al-Kharj C3
Al-Medina A2–B3
Al-Qasim B2–B3
An-Nafud (desert) B2
Aqaba A2
Arabian Sea D4–D5
Ar'ar B2
Ar-Riyadh B2–C4
Ash Sharqiyah (Eastern
     Province) B2–D4
Asir (province) B4
Asir (region) B4
Asir Mountains B4
At-Taif B3

Baghdad B1
Bahrain C3
Basra C2
Buraydah B3

Dhahran C3
Djibouti B5
Doha D3

Egypt A2–A3

Eritrea A4–B5
Ethiopia A5–B5

Gulf of Aden B5–C5
Gulf of Aqaba A2
Gulf of Suez A2

Hafr Al-Batin C2
Ha'il B2
Ha'il (province) B2–B3
Hijaz (region) A3
Hijaz Mountains A2-A3

Iran C1–D3
Iraq B1–C2
Israel A1–A2

Jabal Sawda' B4
Jabal Tuwayq Mountains
     C3–C4
Jiddah A3
Jizan B4
Jizan (province) B4
Jordan A1–B2

Kuwait C2

Lebanon A1

Madain Saleh (ruins) A2
Mecca B3
Mecca (province)
     A3–B4
Medina B3

Mediterranean Sea A1–A2
Mina B3
Mount Arafat B3

Najd (region) B2–B3
Najran B4
Najran (province) B4–C4

Oman D3-D4

Persian Gulf C2–D3

Qatar C3–D3

Ras Al-Khafji C2
Ras Tanura C2
Red Sea A2–B5
Riyadh C3
Rub Al-Khali (Empty
     Quarter) C4–D4

Sakakah B2
Sinai Peninsula A2
Somalia B5–D5
Strait of Hormuz D2–D3
Sudan A3–A5
Suez Canal A2
Syria A1–B1

Tabuk A2
Tabuk (province) A2–B3
Tihamah (plain) B4

United Arab Emirates D3

Yanbu Al-Bahr A3
Yemen B4–D5

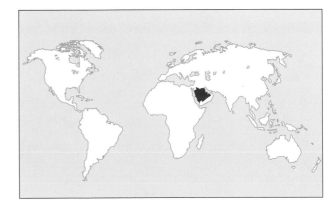

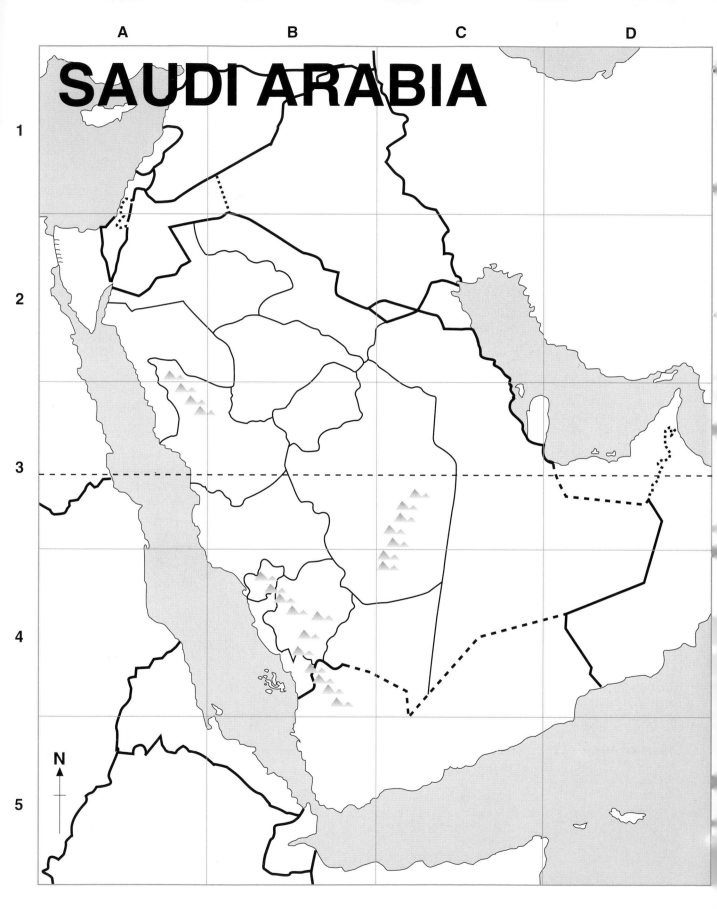

SAUDI ARABIA

How Is Your Geography?

Learning to identify the main geographical areas and points of a country can be challenging. Although it may seem difficult at first to memorize the locations and spellings of major cities or the names of mountain ranges, rivers, deserts, lakes, and other prominent physical features, the end result of this effort can be very rewarding. Places you previously did not know existed will suddenly come to life when referred to in world news, whether in newspapers, television reports, or other books and reference sources. This knowledge will make you feel a bit closer to the rest of the world, with its fascinating variety of cultures and physical geography.

Used in a classroom setting, the instructor can make duplicates of this map using a copy machine. (PLEASE DO NOT WRITE IN THIS BOOK!) Students can then fill in any requested information on their individual map copies. Used one-on-one, the student can also make copies of the map on a copy machine and use them as a study tool. The student can practice identifying place names and geographical features on his or her own.

Above: **A camel train crosses the Arabian Desert.**

Saudi Arabia at a Glance

Official Name	Kingdom of Saudi Arabia
Capital	Riyadh
Official Language	Arabic (English is widely spoken in business.)
Population	22,757,092 (July 2001 estimate)
Land area	865,000 square miles (2,240,350 square km)
Provinces	Al-Bahah, Al-Hudud ash Shamaliyah, Al-Jawf, Al-Medina, Al-Qasim, Ar-Riyadh, Ash Sharqiyah (Eastern Province), Asir, Ha'il, Jizan, Mecca, Najran, Tabuk
Highest Point	Jabal Sawda' 10,279 feet (3,133 m)
Major Bodies of Water	Persian Gulf, Red Sea
Type of Government	Monarchy
Government Leader	King Fahd Bin Abd Al-Aziz Al-Saud
Major Cities	Jiddah, Mecca, Medina, Riyadh, Yanbu Al-Bahr
Holy Sites	Mecca and Medina
Official Religion	Islam
Public Holidays	Eid Al-Fitr (date varies according to Islamic lunar calendar)
	Eid Al-Adha (date varies according to Islamic lunar calendar)
	Unification of the Kingdom (September 23)
Natural Resources	Petroleum, natural gas, iron ore, gold, copper
Major Industries	Oil and petroleum production
Principal Trade Partners	United States, Japan, United Kingdom, Singapore, France
Literacy	Women, 50 percent; men, 72 percent (2001)
GDP	$232 billion; $10,500 per capita (2000 estimate)
Life Expectancy	Women, seventy; men, sixty-six (2001)
Currency	Saudi riyal (3.75 riyals = U.S. $1, fixed rate since June 1986)

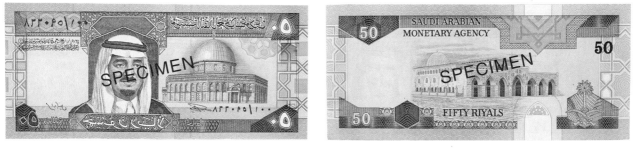

Opposite: **A Saudi family leaves the Masmak Fortress in Riyadh after a day's visit.**

Glossary

Arabic Vocabulary

abayah (ah-BYE-ah): a long, black gown and veil worn by Saudi women that completely covers their bodies and hair.

agal (oh-GAHL): a double cord that holds men's gutras in place.

al-batheeth (ahl-bah-TEETH): a sweet, or candy, made from dates.

ardha (AHR-dah): a men's sword dance; the Saudi national dance.

baba ganoush (BAH-bah GAH-noozh): a dip made from roasted eggplant.

della (DEH-lah): Arabian coffee pots.

Eid Al-Adha (EED ahl-ahd-HAH): a Muslim feast that remembers Abraham's willingness to sacrifice his son, Ishmael.

Eid Al-Fitr (EED ahl-feetr): Muslim feast celebrating the end of Ramadan.

finjan (FEEN-jahn): a game in which the player must uncover a stone that is hidden under one of twelve cups.

gahwa (GAH-hwah): a thick, strong coffee popular in Saudi Arabia.

gutra (GOH-trah): a veil-like head cloth worn by Saudi men.

hajj (HYE-ch): the fifth pillar of Islam. Every Muslim must try to make a pilgrimage to the holy city of Mecca at least once during his or her lifetime.

hasaa al-gareesh (HEE-sah ahl-gah-REESH): wheat soup.

Kabah (KAH-bah): the square building that contains the stone Muslims believe is a part of Abraham's original temple.

khboz (HOH-boes): a flat bread.

kibbeh (KEEB-beh): deep-fried balls of lamb, wheat, and spices.

kiswah (KEES-wah): a cloth that covers the Kabah.

labbayk (lah-bah-YEEK): a profession of faith, which means, "I am here."

mahbash (MAH-bahsh): a pestle used to grind coffee beans.

mahmasa (MAH-hah-mah-sah): an iron pan used to roast coffee beans.

majlis (MITE-jlees): a public audience, during which Saudi citizens meet with their leaders to discuss issues or to petition them.

Majlis Al-Shura (MITE-jlees ahl-SHOE-rah): a special consultative council formed by King Fahd in 1993.

matawwa (moo-TAH-wear): Saudi Arabia's religious police who make sure the laws of Islam are obeyed.

mensaf (MAHN-sahf): a lamb dish.

meza (meh-ZAH): small appetizers.

mishlah (meesh-LAH-hah): a long, white, brown, or black, gold-trimmed cloak that Saudi men sometimes wear over their thobes.

muhammar (mah-HAHM-ahr): sweet rice.

oud (OOD): a gourd-shaped, stringed instrument.

Qur'an (kor-AHN): the sacred book of Islam, as told by Allah to Muhammad.

Ramadan (rah-mah-DAHN): the ninth month of the Islamic lunar calendar.

rebaba (reh-BAH-bah): a one-stringed instrument played by the Bedouin.

rigg (REEG): a kind of tambourine.

Rub Al-Khali (roob ahl-HAH-lee): the world's largest sand desert, also called the Empty Quarter.

sabkha (SOB-hah): salt flats.

salah (sah-LAH): the second pillar of Islam, declaring that Muslims must pray five times each day, facing the holy Kabah at Mecca.

sawm (SOWM): the fourth pillar of Islam, dictating that during the month of Ramadan, Muslims must not eat, drink, or have sexual relations between sunrise and sunset.

shahada (shee-HAH-daht): the first pillar of Islam, the declaration of faith that there is no god but Allah and Muhammad is his messenger.

shari'a (shah-REE-ah): Islamic holy law.

Shawal (shah-WAHL): the tenth month of the Islamic lunar calendar.

souq (SOOK): a market; the Arab equivalent of a Western shopping mall.

sura (SOO-rah): chapters of the Qur'an.

tagia (tahg-EE-ah): a small, white skullcap that Saudi men wear.

tawle (tah-LEE): the game of backgammon.

thobe (THOE-b): a long, white robe worn by Saudi men.

ulema (oo-leh-MAH): a council of Muslim religious leaders.

Wahhabi (wah-HAH-bee): an Islamic sect that believes in a literal interpretation of the Qur'an.

zakat (zah-KAHT): the third pillar of Islam, which says Muslims must give to the poor in their community.

Zul Hijjah (zool HEE-jah): the twelfth month of the Islamic lunar calendar.

English Vocabulary

adobe: sun-dried bricks.

allegiance: strong loyalty to a group, cause, or country.

amputation: the act of cutting off a limb.

arbitrary: based on personal judgment, often marked by a misuse of power, rather than on necessity or truth.

archaeology: the study of human artifacts.

arid: extremely dry; lacking in moisture or rainfall.

artesian wells: wells found below layers of rock in which water under pressure rises naturally to Earth's surface.

deploy: to send or place military troops in preparation for battle.

dromedary: camel.

embalm: to preserve or protect from decay.

guerrilla warfare: the use of surprise attacks by small groups of soldiers to fight a much larger enemy force.

hereditary: passed down from one generation to the next.

literacy: the state of being able to read and write.

minaret: a high tower on a mosque from which Muslims are called to prayer five times a day.

mosque: a Muslim place of worship.

nomads: people who roam from place to place.

oryx: a horned, antelopelike animal that roams the deserts of Saudi Arabia.

pilgrimage: a journey to a shrine or sacred place.

tactician: a person who plans military strategy.

terrain: the physical features of an area of land.

More Books to Read

Saudi Arabia. Countries: Faces and Places series. Bob Temple (Child's World)

Saudi Arabia. Country Fact Files series. Susannah Honeyman (Raintree Steck-Vaughn)

Saudi Arabia. Cultures of the World series. Hunt Janin (Benchmark Books)

Saudi Arabia. Enchantment of the World series. Leila Merrell Foster (Children's Press)

Saudi Arabia. Festivals of the World series. Maria O'Shea (Gareth Stevens)

Saudi Arabia. Globe-Trotters Club series. Laurie Halse Anderson and Helga Jones
    (Carolrhoda Books)

Saudi Arabia. Major World Nations series. Martin Mulloy (Chelsea House)

Saudi Arabia. True Books series. Wende Fazio (Children's Press)

Saudi Arabia in Pictures. Visual Geography series. Eugene Gordon
    (Lerner Publications Company)

Videos

History Makers: Lawrence of Arabia. (Madacy Entertainment)

National Geographic's Arabia: Sand, Sea & Sky. (National Geographic)

World Almanac Video: Ancient Arabia. (Choices, Inc.)

Web Sites

www.arab.net/saudi/saudi_contents.html

www.castle-hill-press.com/teweb/life/biog.htm

www.iad.org/

www.saudicaves.com/index.html

www.saudiembassy.net/profile/saudi-profile.html

www.un.int/saudiarabia/sa-prfl.htm

Due to the dynamic nature of the Internet, some web sites stay current longer than others. To find additional web sites, use a reliable search engine with one or more of the following keywords to help you locate information on Saudi Arabia. Keywords: *Bedouin, desalination plants, desert, hajj, Islam, T. E. Lawrence, Mecca (Makkah), Muhammad, oil.*

Index